Y0-BQQ-987

POLITICAL SYSTEMS, STRUCTURES, AND FUNCTIONS

POLITICAL SYSTEMS, STRUCTURES, AND FUNCTIONS

EDITED BY BRIAN DUIGNAN, SENIOR EDITOR, RELIGION AND PHILOSOPHY

Britannica®
Educational Publishing

IN ASSOCIATION WITH

ROSEN
EDUCATIONAL SERVICES

Published in 2013 by Britannica Educational Publishing
(a trademark of Encyclopædia Britannica, Inc.)
in association with Rosen Educational Services, LLC
29 East 21st Street, New York, NY 10010.

Distributed exclusively by Rosen Educational Services.
For a listing of additional Britannica Educational Publishing titles, call toll free (800) 237-9932.

First Edition

Britannica Educational Publishing
J.E. Luebering: Senior Manager
Adam Augustyn, Assistant Manager
Marilyn L. Barton: Senior Coordinator, Production Control
Steven Bosco: Director, Editorial Technologies
Lisa S. Braucher: Senior Producer and Data Editor
Yvette Charboneau: Senior Copy Editor
Kathy Nakamura: Manager, Media Acquisition
Brian Duignan: Senior Editor, Religion and Philosophy

Rosen Educational Services
Jeanne Nagle: Senior Editor
Nelson Sá: Art Director
Cindy Reiman: Photography Manager
Brian Garvey: Designer, Cover Design
Introduction by Brian Duignan

Library of Congress Cataloging-in-Publication Data

Political systems, structures, and functions/edited by Brian Duignan.—1st ed.
    p. cm.—(Governance: power, politics, and participation)
"In association with Britannica Educational Publishing, Rosen Educational Services."
Includes bibliographical references and index.
ISBN 978-1-61530-700-5 (library binding)
1. Comparative government. I. Duignan, Brian.
JF51.P638 2012
320.3—dc23

2011051613

Manufactured in the United States of America

On the cover, pp. i, iii (top): Flags of many countries flying outside the United Nations building in New York City. *Shutterstock.com*

On the cover (centre), pp. ii (centre), iii (centre), 1, 36, 58, 94, 116, 134, 137, 139, 141: Columns that make up the portico of the United States Supreme Court. © *www.istockphoto.com/Jeremy Edwards*

On the cover, pp. i, iii (bottom): Rows of seats awaiting members of the European Parliament, an elected legislative body of the European Union. © *www.istockphoto.com/Jakub Wójtowicz*

CONTENTS

10

29

47

120

130

INTRODUCTION

The ancient Greek philosopher Aristotle famously observed that "man is a political animal." By this he meant that it is natural and, indeed, necessary, for human beings to live together in political communities, or states. It is necessary that they do so in part because states are the only kind of community that is self-sufficient and therefore capable of ensuring the long-term survival of individual humans. More importantly, states are also necessary because they are the only kind of community in which it is possible to lead a life of human flourishing,

Illustration of a public market in ancient Greece. Aristotle emphasized the role of the city-state in enabling its citizens to flourish. Nick Hewetson/ Getty Images

characterized by the full development and exercise of the intellectual and moral virtues. Indeed, the chief purpose of a well-run state, in Aristotle's view, is to enable its citizens to lead good lives.

This book introduces the major political systems of the world, giving readers an opportunity to deepen their understanding of the governments under which they live. Discussed herein are the common and distinguishing structures, functions, and processes of various political systems, as well as the history of their study, from ancient times to the present.

The kind of state Aristotle had in mind was the polis, or city-state, the most common form of political organization in ancient Greece. In his treatise the *Politics*, Aristotle undertook to survey the various forms of government exemplified in the city-states, to classify those forms systematically, to discover the conditions necessary for political stability and the causes of violent political change (revolutions), and to identify which form (or forms) were most conducive to human flourishing. His answer to the last question was that monarchy is the best form of government if the monarch and his family are of excellent ability and moral character. Otherwise, aristocracy is best, but again only if the ruling class is well-qualified. Because these conditions are infrequently attained in reality, however, in practice the best form of government is a mixture of aristocracy and democracy, which he called "polity." (It is an idiosyncracy of Aristotle's system that democracy in its pure form is more or less equivalent to anarchy, or mob rule.) In any event, a well-run state must be based on the rule of law and have political and economic institutions that respect basic principles of justice.

For his systematic empirical researches into the forms of government of his day, Aristotle is rightly regarded as the first political scientist in history. Although his classification scheme did not explicitly encompass political organizations larger than the city-state—some of which, including leagues and empires, existed in the ancient world—it was influential among political theorists and philosophers for nearly two millennia. Beginning in the 17th century, other schemes were developed (notably by Montesquieu) to describe and evaluate the forms of government of nation-states, which had gradually coalesced in Europe in the 15th and 16th centuries. With the emergence of the empirical discipline of political science in the 19th century, schemes of increasing complexity, taking into greater account the structures and functions of government, became commonplace.

Today there is an entire field of political science, known as comparative politics, that is devoted to analyzing and classifying different forms of government. Its objects of study are more properly called political systems, however, because they comprise not only the formal legal institutions through which nations are governed (that is, those institutions that may be established in a written or unwritten constitution) but also various informal or unofficial structures and processes, as well as the ways in which governments of all forms interact with aspects of the nation's economy, society, and culture. Contemporary classifications of political systems may be based, as Aristotle's was, on the number and aims of their rulers—yielding, in Aristotle's classification, the basic forms of monarchy versus tyranny; aristocracy versus oligarchy; and democracy (mob rule) versus polity. Or they may emphasize key institutions (presidential and parliamentary systems), principles of authority or legitimate power (charismatic, traditional, and rational-legal systems), forms of economic organization (capitalist and socialist systems), the economic class of rulers (bourgeois and feudal systems), the manner in which political power is transferred (by heredity, by election, by constitutional rule, or by force), the manner in which political power is exercised and controlled (autocratic and nonautocratic systems), or the "stage of development" of the system in question (traditional and modern systems).

Although they may be classified and referred to in different ways, the basic kinds of political system in existence since the early 20th century are monarchy, dictatorship (encompassing totalitarian systems as well as military dictatorships), oligarchy, and constitutional democracy. Some political systems incorporate elements of more than one basic kind, as in the constitutional monarchies of some European countries, which may have both a king or a queen (with limited powers) and a democratically elected prime minister or president. In other countries, the political system is formally democratic but in practice partly or wholly dictatorial or oligarchic, as in China, Russia, and communist North Korea.

As indicated, the nation-state or country is now the most common and important kind of political organization in the world, though there remain many other kinds, including city-states (e.g., the Vatican), leagues (e.g., the Arab League), federations (e.g., the Commonwealth of Nations), and various other supranational organizations, such as the United Nations (UN), the European Union (EU), and the North Atlantic Treaty Organization (NATO).

National political systems typically comprise more than one level of government. In addition to the national or central government, for example, there may be regional or provincial governments; state governments; county governments; city, town, and village governments; and district or parish governments. Systems in which political authority is shared between a national or central government and governments at one or more lower levels are called federal systems, the oldest of which is that of the United States. Systems in which all authority is exercised or delegated by the national or central government are called unitary systems. The vast majority of national political systems, including those of most European countries, are unitary.

Almost all political systems, no matter what their kind or level, perform three basic kinds of governmental function: executive, legislative, and judicial. The system may in addition comprise separate branches or offices corresponding to each of these functions. The executive function, for example, consists of determining and executing government policy, leading the armed forces (if any), and, in some systems, enforcing laws. The legislative function, as the term suggests, consists of passing legislation, which may or may not require the signature of the chief executive to become law. Typically, legislatures exercise many other important powers, including appropriating money for government activities; selecting (in parliamentary systems) the chief executive; confirming appointments to some executive offices; declaring war; overriding, usually with a supermajority of votes, vetoes of legislation by the chief executive; ratifying treaties or other intergovernmental agreements; and impeaching and trying executive or judicial officers for official misconduct.

The primary judicial function, which is usually performed by a system of courts, consists of adjudicating conflicts between individuals and the state over alleged violations of criminal law or between individuals themselves over alleged violations of civil (private) law. In some systems there may be two or more levels of courts that perform this function, as well as one or more levels that hear appeals of cases from other courts. In some systems there is a separate set of courts whose role is to decide questions of constitutional interpretation that have arisen in other cases or that have been specially brought before it; in other systems, any court may rule on constitutional questions. In the United States and several other countries, most courts have the power of judicial review, meaning that they can declare laws and administrative regulations constitutional or unconstitutional. In the latter case, the law becomes invalid and is no longer enforceable.

Some supranational political systems also carry out judicial functions through a special set of courts. In the United Nations system, for example, the International Court of Justice (also called the World Court) adjudicates disputes between countries and may try individuals as well as countries for violations of international law.

The basic executive, legislative, and judicial functions encompass a variety of cross-cutting and more specific functions that all governments must perform. They include self-preservation (i.e., preservation of the political system or of the state itself), resolution of conflicts between private interests, regulation of the economy, protection of individual rights and freedoms, and provision of basic goods and services. The imperative of self-preservation may require maintaining armed forces and foreign-intelligence agencies to guard against external enemies and deploying police forces and domestic-intelligence agencies to maintain order and to root out internal enemies. Self-preservation may also entail the use of the educational system and the mass media to instill and reinforce an official ideology or to discourage acceptance of a competing ideology.

In constitutional democracies, conflicts between private interests can be managed through participation in the political process (in order to elect leaders who will favor one interest or another or to influence incumbents to do the same). To the latter end, interest groups may establish legal organizations to lobby for or against certain policies or laws. Political parties usually represent a broad range of private interests, which they attempt to promote by gaining control of government, either by themselves or in coalitions with other parties.

All political systems incorporate some form of economic regulation, and indeed some classifications of political systems are based on the nature or extent of such regulation. (Although laissez-faire political systems exist as a hypothetical category in some classifications, no such system has ever existed in reality.) In capitalist political systems, typical forms of economic regulation include antitrust laws, environmental regulations, worker health and safety laws, minimum-wage laws, antidiscrimination laws, banking and financial-industry regulations, and laws protecting the right of workers to form unions.

In most countries, including the United States, individual rights and freedoms are guaranteed against government infringement by the constitution—in the U.S. case by the

Bill of Rights and some later amendments. Political systems differ widely, however, in what rights and freedoms they recognize as fundamental. For example, while freedom of speech and association and the right to privacy are almost universally accepted, the rights to education, employment, health care, and recreation are not. Similarly, the Second Amendment right to "keep and bear arms" (which the U.S. Supreme Court has interpreted to mean the individual right to possess and carry guns) is recognized in few countries other than the United States.

In capitalist political systems there is generally a distinction between public and private services, the former being those performed or directed by the government and the latter being those performed by private businesses. The rationale for observing the distinction is usually the simple one that there are some necessary services that cannot be adequately provided to sufficient numbers of people at a reasonable cost by private means. In most systems these are assumed to include police and fire protection, education, health care or health insurance, emergency and disaster services, power services, and postal services, among many others.

Although political systems have been studied and classified since ancient times, there is still much to be learned about their elements and characteristics, their origins and development, and, in the case of contemporary systems, their likely future. Anyone who is interested in exploring what is known—and unknown—about political systems and governments would do well to start with this book.

CHAPTER 1

Political Systems

A political system is the set of formal legal institutions that constitute a "government" or a "state." This is the definition adopted by many studies of the legal or constitutional arrangements of advanced political orders. More broadly defined, however, the term comprehends actual as well as prescribed forms of political behaviour; not only the legal organization of the state but also the reality of how the state functions. Still more broadly defined, the political system is seen as a set of "processes of interaction" or as a subsystem of the social system interacting with other nonpolitical subsystems, such as the economic system. This points to the importance of informal socio-political processes and emphasizes the study of political development.

Traditional legal or constitutional analysis, using the first definition, has produced a huge body of literature on governmental structures, many of the specialized terms that are a part of the traditional vocabulary of political science, and several instructive classifying schemes. Similarly, empirical analysis of political processes and the effort to identify the underlying realities of governmental forms have yielded a rich store of data and an important body of comparative theory. The third definition has inspired much scholarly work that employs new kinds of data, new terms, and some new concepts and categories of analysis. The discussion in this book draws on all three approaches to the study of political systems.

The most important type of political system in the modern world is the nation-state. The world today is divided territorially into more than 190 countries, in each of which a national government claims to exercise sovereignty—or the power of final authority—and seeks to compel obedience to its will by its citizens. This fact of the world's political organization suggests the distinction among supranational, national, and subnational political systems.

SUPRANATIONAL POLITICAL SYSTEMS

The formation of supranational relationships is a principal result of the division of the world into a number of separate national entities, or states, that have contact with one another, share goals or needs, and face common threats. In some cases, as in many alliances, these relationships are short-lived and fail to result in significant institutional development. In other cases, they lead to interstate organizations and supranational systems. The following discussion examines several types of supranational political systems, together with historical and contemporary examples of each.

EMPIRES

Because they are composed of peoples of different cultures and ethnic backgrounds, all empires are ultimately held together by coercion and the threat of forcible reconquest. Imposing their rule on diverse political structures, they are characterized by the centralization of power and the absence of effective representation of their component parts. Although force is thus the primary instrument of imperial rule, it is also true that history records many cases of multiethnic empires that were governed peaceably for considerable periods and were often quite successful in maintaining order within their boundaries. The history of the ancient world is the history of great empires—Egypt, China, Persia, and imperial Rome—whose autocratic regimes provided relatively stable government for many subject peoples in immense territories over many centuries. Based on military force and religious belief, the ancient despotisms were legitimized also by their achievements in building great bureaucratic and legal structures, in developing vast irrigation and road systems, and in providing the conditions for the support of high civilizations. Enhancing and transcending all other political structures in their sphere, they could claim to function as effective schemes of universal order.

In contrast to the empires of the ancient world, the colonial empires of more recent times fell far short of universal status. In part, these modern European empires were made up of "colonies" in the original Greek sense. Peopled by immigrants from the mother country, the colonies usually established political structures similar to those of the metropolitan centre and were often able to exercise a substantial measure of self-government. In part, also, the European empires were composed of territories inhabited by indigenous populations and administered by imperial bureaucracies. The government of these territories was generally more coercive than in the European colonies and more concerned with protection and supervision of the commercial, industrial, and other exploitative interests of the imperial power.

The disintegration of these empires occurred with astonishing speed. The two world wars of the 20th century sapped the power of the metropolitan centres, while their own doctrines of democracy, equality, and self-determination undermined the principle of imperial rule. Powers such as Britain and France found it increasingly difficult to resist claims to independence couched

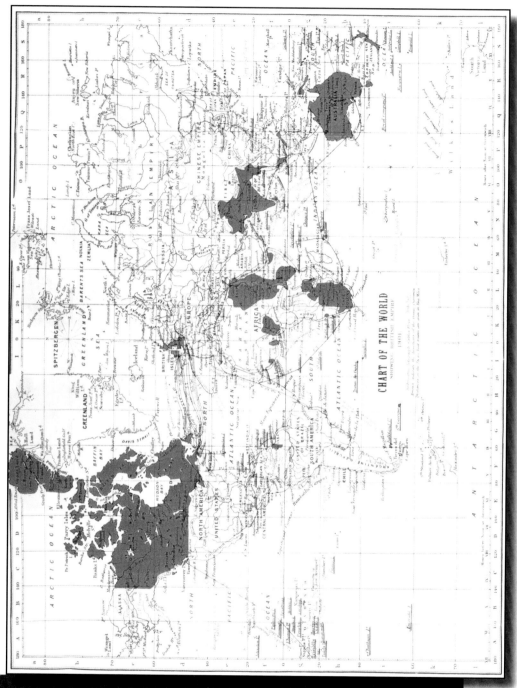

Worldview map showing the extent of the British Empire in 1901 (indicated in red). © Visual & Written/SuperStock

in terms of the representative concepts on which their home governments were based, and they lacked the military and economic strength to continue their rule over restive indigenous populations. In the two decades after 1945, nearly all the major colonial territories won their independence. The great colonial empires that had once ruled more than half the world were finally dismembered.

LEAGUES

One of the commonest forms of supranational organization in history is that of leagues, generally composed of states seeking to resist some common military or economic threat by combining their forces. This was the case with the early city leagues, such as the Achaean and Aetolian leagues in ancient Greece and the Hanseatic and the Swabian leagues in late-medieval Europe, and to a great extent it was the case with the 20th-century League of Nations. Other common features of leagues include the existence of some form of charter or agreement among the member states, an assembly of representatives of the constituent members, an executive organ for the implementation of the decisions of the assembly of representatives, and an arbitral or judicial body for adjudicating disputes.

The League of Nations was one of the great experiments in supranational organization of the 20th century and the predecessor in several important respects of the United Nations. The Covenant of the League was drafted by a special commission of the Peace Conference after World War I, with Pres. Woodrow Wilson of the United States as its leading advocate, and approved by a plenary conference of the victorious powers in 1919. The initial membership of the League consisted of 20 states; the United States failed to join the League. By 1928 the organization had a total membership of 54.

ACHAEAN LEAGUE

The Achaean League was a 3rd-century-BCE confederation of the towns of Achaea (a region on the northern coast of the Peloponnese peninsula) in ancient Greece. The 12 Achaean cities had organized a league by the 4th century BCE to protect themselves against piratical raids from across the Corinthian Gulf, but this league fell apart after the death of Alexander the Great. The 10 surviving cities renewed their alliance in 280 BCE, and under the leadership of Aratus of Sicyon, the league gained strength by the inclusion of his city, and later other non-Achaean cities, on equal terms.

The league's activity initially centred on the expulsion of the Macedonians and the restoration of Greek rule in the Peloponnese. After this was successfully accomplished in about 228 BCE, Achaea faced the danger of complete disintegration before the assaults of the Spartan king Cleomenes III, who also aimed at control of the Peloponnese. To counteract the Spartan threat, Aratus allied the league with Macedon, and Antigonus III Doson of Macedon and his troops subdued Sparta, making it a Macedonian ally and renewing the Macedonian hold over Greece (224–221). In the Second Macedonian War, Achaea joined Rome (198) in an alliance against Macedon, and this new policy led to the incorporation of nearly the whole Peloponnese into the Achaean League. But the league's success eventually resulted in friction with both Sparta (which had been drafted into the league in 192) and with expansionist Rome, and war broke out between the league and Rome in 146 BCE. Rome was soon victorious, and it dissolved the Achaean League in the same year. A smaller league, however, was set up soon afterward and continued into the Roman imperial age.

At the head of the Achaean League were two generals (*strategoi*) until a single general was substituted in 255 BCE. The general was the annually elected head of the league's army, and a particular general could not be immediately reelected. The general headed the league's administrative board, whose 10 members in turn presided over the various city-states' representative councils and assemblies. These bodies of citizenry could vote on matters submitted to them by the general. The minimum voting age in the assemblies was 30 years of age.

Under the Achaean League's federal constitution, its city-state members had almost complete autonomy within the framework of the league's central administration. Only matters of foreign policy, war, and federal taxes were referred to the general and the board for decision making.

The machinery of the League consisted of an Assembly of all the member countries, acting through agents of their governments; a council on which the great powers were permanently represented and to which the other member powers were elected by the Assembly for three-year terms; a Secretariat to administer the internal affairs of the League; and a number of specialized agencies, such as the International Labour Organisation, that were responsible for implementing various economic and humanitarian programs on an international basis. The Covenant required that international disputes be submitted to peaceful settlement with a provision for adjudication or arbitration by the Permanent Court of International Justice or for intervention by the Council of the League. The Covenant also provided for the use of financial and economic penalties, such as embargoes, to enforce the decisions of the League and for joint military action against convicted aggressors. In practice, however, the League failed its most important tests and was unable to master the crises that led to World War II and its own collapse.

THE UNITED NATIONS

The United Nations is a voluntary association of most of the world's nation-states. Its membership had grown from an original 51 states to more than 190 by the early 21st century. (The government of the People's Republic of China was admitted in place of the government of Taiwan in 1971.) The United Nations was founded in 1945 at a conference in San Francisco that was attended by representatives of all the countries that had declared war on Germany or Japan. The purposes of the organization are declared in its Charter to be the maintenance of international peace and security, the development of friendly relations among states, and international cooperation in solving the political, economic, social, cultural, and humanitarian problems of the world. Its organizational structure consists of a Security Council of five permanent members (China, France, Russia, the United Kingdom, and the United States) and 10 nonpermanent members elected for two-year terms, a General Assembly, a secretary-general and a Secretariat, an Economic and Social Council, a Trusteeship Council, and the International Court of Justice, also called the World Court. Attached to the United Nations are a number of specialized agencies, including the Food and Agriculture Organization, the International Atomic Energy Agency, the International Civil Aviation Organization, the International Labour Organisation, the International Monetary Fund, the International Telecommunications Union, the Universal Postal Union, the United Nations Educational, Scientific and Cultural Organization, the World Health Organization, and the International Bank for Reconstruction and Development (World Bank).

Aside from the rather generally stated and decidedly elusive aims of the Charter, the member states of the United Nations cannot be said to have any common goal, and they have often failed to unify in the face of common external threats to security. There also has been difficulty in reaching and implementing decisions. Two different formulas are employed for voting in the two principal organs, the General Assembly and the Security Council. In the General Assembly a two-thirds majority decides on important matters, but, since the Assembly's decisions are not binding and are merely recommendations, this qualified majority principle must be viewed as of little significance. Although, on the other hand, the decisions of the Security Council may be binding, a unanimous vote of all five of the permanent members joined by the votes of at least four of the nonpermanent members is required. Whenever important questions of peace and security are at stake, it has rarely been possible to achieve agreement among the five great powers of the council. Although these difficulties might be fatal to the survival of many supranational organizations, they are not in fact totally debilitating for the United Nations. The United Nations continues to serve as a very important forum for international debate and negotiation.

CONFEDERATIONS AND FEDERATIONS

Confederations are voluntary associations of independent states that, to secure some common purpose, agree to certain limitations on their freedom of action and establish some joint machinery of consultation or deliberation. Limitations on the member states may be as trivial as an acknowledgment of their duty to consult with each other before taking some independent action or as significant as the obligation to be bound by majority decisions of the member states.

Confederations usually fail to provide for an effective executive authority and lack viable central governments. Their member states typically retain their separate

British diplomat Arthur Balfour (standing, left) addressing the first meeting of the Council of the League of Nations in 1920. A. R. Coster/Hulton Archive/Getty Images

military establishments and separate diplomatic representation, and members are generally accorded equal status with an acknowledged right of secession from the confederation. The term *federation* is used to refer to groupings of states, often on a regional basis, that establish central executive machinery to implement policies or to supervise joint activities. In some cases such groupings are motivated primarily by political or economic concerns. In others, military objectives are paramount.

Historically, confederations have often proved to be a first or second step toward the establishment of a national state, usually as a federal union. Thus, the federal union of modern Switzerland was preceded by a confederation of the Swiss cantons; Germany's modern federal arrangements may be traced to the German Confederation of the 19th century (the Deutsche Bund); and the federal constitution of the United States is the successor to the government of the Articles of Confederation. In some other cases, confederations have replaced more centralized arrangements, as, for example, when empires disintegrate and are replaced by voluntary associations of their former colonies. The Commonwealth (also called the Commonwealth of Nations; originally called the British Commonwealth) and the former French Community are cases of this type.

An example of confederal arrangements that gave birth to a federal union is the Articles of Confederation (1781–89), which preceded the Constitution of the United States. The Articles established a Congress of the confederation as a unicameral assembly of ambassadors from the 13 states, each possessing a single vote. The Congress was authorized to appoint an executive committee of states

> *to execute, in the recess of Congress, such of the powers of Congress as the United States, in Congress assembled, by the consent of nine States, shall from time to time think expedient to vest them with.*

In turn, the committee of states could appoint a presiding officer or president for a term of one year. The Congress could also appoint such other committees and "civil officers as may be necessary for managing the general affairs of the United States" and was given the authority to serve as "the last resort or appeal in all disputes and differences, now subsisting or that hereafter may arise between two or more states."

Although the Congress was given authority in important areas such as the regulation of foreign affairs, the establishment of coinage and weights and measures, the appointment of officers in the confederation's land and naval forces, and the issuance of bills of credit, all its powers were in fact dependent for their enforcement upon the states. The Congress lacked both an independent source of revenue and the executive machinery to enforce its will directly upon individuals. As the language of the Articles summarized the situation,

> *each State retains its sovereignty, freedom and independence, and every power, jurisdiction and right, which is not by this Confederation expressly delegated to the United States in Congress assembled.*

The Commonwealth is an example of a confederation born as the result of the decentralization and eventual disintegration of an empire. The original members in 1931 were the United Kingdom, Australia, Canada, the Irish Free State (Ireland), Newfoundland, New Zealand, and the Union of South Africa. In 1949 Newfoundland became a province of Canada, and Ireland withdrew from the Commonwealth. In 1961 South Africa also withdrew from the organization, although it rejoined in 1994. Several new Commonwealth members in the latter half of the 20th century were newly independent former British colonies, such as Malaysia (1957), Cyprus (1961), Kiribati (1979), and Brunei (1984). Namibia joined in 1990 upon gaining independence from South Africa. By the early 21st century, the Commonwealth had grown to include more than 50 members. It also had embraced countries—i.e., Mozambique (1995) and Rwanda (2009)—that lacked colonial ties to Britain.

The Statute of Westminster (1931) established that all members were equal in status. The London Declaration (1949) permitted members to be republics, although all member countries must recognize the British monarch as the symbolic head of the Commonwealth.

Commonwealth governments are represented in the capitals of other Commonwealth countries by high commissioners equal in status to ambassadors. The Commonwealth Secretariat organizes meetings, keeps the membership informed, and implements its collective decisions. Member countries have benefited from trade privileges, technical assistance, and educational exchanges. In the second half of the 20th century, the Commonwealth formulated a mission of promoting democracy, economic development, and human rights.

The European Union (EU) is a supranational organization that, while resisting strict classification as either a confederation or a federation, has both confederal and federal aspects. Its predecessor, the European Communities (EC)—comprising the European Coal and Steel Community, established in 1952; the European Economic Community (Common Market), established in 1958; and the European Atomic Energy Community (Euratom)—quickly developed executive machinery

Flag of the European Union. Encyclopædia Britannica.

exercising significant regulatory and directive authority over the governments and private business firms of the member countries. When the communities were subsumed under the EU in 1993, the EU inherited this executive authority. Yet, despite the EU's central executive machinery (a key feature of a federal system), each of the member governments retains a substantial measure of national sovereignty—an important aspect of confederal arrangements.

The North Atlantic Treaty Organization (NATO), a military alliance established in April 1949, also is endowed with complex and permanent executive machinery, employing multilateral procedures and involving the continuous elaboration of plans for the conduct of joint military action by its member states. As stated in its treaty, the purpose of NATO is to maintain the security of the North Atlantic area by exercise of the right of collective security recognized in the Charter of the United Nations. An impressive array of institutional mechanisms was established—including a secretary-general and a permanent staff, a council, a military command structure, and liaison staffs—and an ongoing system of collaboration in planning and joint military exercises was brought into being. With the continued development of its organization, NATO gradually added a number of economic and cultural activities to its functions until it came to possess several of the features of a multipurpose supranational organization. As in the EU, however, membership in NATO does not override national sovereignty.

NATIONAL POLITICAL SYSTEMS

The term *nation-state* is used so commonly and yet defined so variously. Usage of the term in this book will be done with some precision, as will historical and contemporary examples of nation-states.

To begin with, there is no single basis upon which such systems are established. Many states were formed at a point in time when a people sharing a common history, culture, and language discovered a sense of identity. This was true in the cases of England and France, for example, which were the first nation-states to emerge in the modern period, and of Italy and Germany, which were established as nation-states in the 19th century. In contrast, however, other states, such as India, the Soviet Union, and Switzerland, came into existence without a common basis in ethnicity, culture, or language.

It must also be emphasized that contemporary nation-states are creations of different historical periods and of varied circumstances. Before the close of the 19th century, the effective mobilization of governmental powers on a national basis had occurred only in Europe, the United States, and Japan. It was not until the 20th century and the collapse of the Ottoman, Habsburg, French, and British empires that the bulk of the world could be organized on a national basis. This transformation continued with the dissolution of the Soviet Union, which ceased to exist in 1991, and of Yugoslavia, which finally disappeared in 2003.

In 1920 the League of Nations had recognized seven nation-states as "Great Powers"—the United Kingdom, France, the United States, Germany, Italy, Japan, and Russia—and it eventually admitted more than 40 other states to membership. Its successor, the United Nations, had more than 190 member states in the early 21st century. States in the post–Cold War world include the Great Powers—which, along with Canada, now constitute the highly industrialized countries known as the Group of Eight (G8)—and numerous other populous and prominent countries, such as Argentina, Australia, Brazil, China, Egypt, Greece, Hungary, India, Indonesia, Iran, Ireland, Kenya, Mexico, Nigeria, Pakistan, Poland, Saudi Arabia, South Africa, South Korea, Spain, Sweden, Switzerland, Turkey, and Venezuela. Other states range in size from the tiny Pacific island country of Nauru to the vast Central Asian country of Kazakhstan.

The characteristics that qualify these variously composed and historically differing entities as nation-states and distinguish them from other forms of social and political organization amount in sum to the independent power to compel obedience from the populations within their territories. The state is, in other words, a territorial association that claims supremacy over all other associations within its boundaries. As an association, the state is peculiar in several respects: membership is compulsory for its citizens, it claims a monopoly of the use of armed force within its borders, and its officers (who are the government of the state) claim the right to act in the name of the land and its people.

A definition of the state in terms only of its powers over its members is not wholly satisfactory, however. Although all states make a claim to supremacy within their boundaries, they differ widely in their ability to make good their claims. States are, in fact, often challenged by competing associations within their boundaries. Their supremacy is often more formal than real, and they are sometimes unable to maintain their existence. Moreover, a definition in terms of power alone ignores the fact that there are great differences among states in the structures they employ for the exercise of power, in the ways they use power, and in the ends to which they turn their power. Some of these differences are explored in the discussion that follows of two general categories of nation-states: the unitary state and the federal state.

Partly from administrative necessity and partly because of the pressures of territorial interests, nearly all modern states provide for some distribution of governmental authority on a territorial basis. Systems in which power is delegated from the central government to subnational units and in which the grant of power may be rescinded at the will of the central government are termed unitary systems. Systems in which a balance is established between two autonomous sets of governments, one national and the other provincial, are termed federal. In federal systems, the provincial units are usually empowered to grant and take away the authority of their own subunits in the same manner as national governments in unitary systems. Thus, although the United States is federally organized at the national level, each of the 50 states is in a unitary relationship to the cities and local governments within its own territory.

UNITARY NATION-STATES

A great majority of all the world's nation-states are unitary systems, including Bulgaria, France, Great Britain, the Netherlands, Japan, Poland, Romania, the Scandinavian countries, Spain, and many of the Latin American and African countries. There are great differences among these unitary states, however, specifically in the institutions and procedures through which their central governments interact with their territorial subunits.

In one type of unitary system, decentralization of power among subnational governments goes so far that in practice, although not in constitutional principle, they resemble federal arrangements. In Great Britain, for example, there are important elements of regional autonomy in the relationship between the national government in London and the governments of Scotland, Wales, and

Northern Ireland, where national assemblies were established in 1999 and assumed some powers previously held exclusively by the central Parliament at Westminster. The complex system of elected local governments is in practice a fixed and fairly formidable part of the apparatus of British government. In other unitary systems of this type, decentralization on a territorial basis is actually provided for constitutionally, and the powers of locally elected officials are prescribed in detail. Thus, the Japanese constitution, for example, specifies certain autonomous functions to be performed by local administrative authorities.

A second type of unitary system makes less provision for territorial decentralization of authority and employs rather strict procedures for the central supervision of locally elected governments. The classic example of this type is pre-1982 France. Until March 1982, when a law on decentralization went into effect, the French administrative system was built around *départements*, each headed by a *préfet*, and subdivisions of the *départements*, termed *arrondissements*, each headed by a *sous-préfet*. The *préfets* and *sous-préfets* were appointed by the government in Paris to serve as agents of the central government and also as the executives of the divisional governments, the *conseils généraux*, which were composed of elected officials. The system thus combined central supervision of local affairs through appointed officials with territorial representation through locally elected governments. Following the passage of the decentralization law, the executive powers of the *préfets* were transferred to the elected *conseils généraux*. Moreover, many functions previously performed by the central government were devolved to the newly created *régions*, which are units of local government that encompass a number of *départements* and that are overseen by directly elected regional councils.

Yet a third type of unitary system provides for only token decentralization. In such cases, the officials responsible for managing the affairs of the territorial subdivisions are appointees of the central government, and the role of locally elected officers is either minimal or nonexistent. Examples of this kind of arrangement include Germany under Adolf Hitler and also several formerly communist countries. The Third Reich was divided into 42 Gaue, each headed by a gauleiter chosen for his personal loyalty to Hitler. In eastern Europe, the people's councils or people's committees were named by the centrally organized communist parties. Their appointment was confirmed by elections in which there was only one slate of candidates.

FEDERAL SYSTEMS

In federal systems, political authority is divided between two autonomous sets of governments, one national and the other subnational, both of which operate directly upon the people. Usually a constitutional division of power is established between the national government, which exercises authority over the whole national territory, and provincial governments, which exercise independent authority within their own territories. Of the eight largest countries in the world by area, seven—Russia, Canada, the United States, Brazil, Australia, India, and Argentina—are organized on a federal basis. (China, the third largest, is a unitary state.) Federal countries also include Austria, Germany, Malaysia, Mexico, Nigeria, Switzerland, and Venezuela.

The governmental structures and political processes found in these federal systems show great variety. One may distinguish, first, a number of systems in which federal arrangements reflect rather clear-cut cultural divisions. A classic case of this type is Switzerland, where the people speak four different languages—German, French, Italian, and Romansh. The Swiss federal system unites 26 historically and culturally different entities, known as cantons and demicantons. The Swiss constitution of 1848, as modified in 1874, converted into the modern federal state a confederation originally formed in the 13th century by the three forest cantons of Uri, Schwyz, and Unterwalden. The principal agencies of federal government are: (1) a bicameral legislature, composed of a National Council representing the people directly and a Council of States representing the constituent members as entities, (2) an executive branch (Federal Council) elected by both houses of the legislature in joint session, and (3) a supreme court that renders decisions on matters affecting cantonal and federal relations.

The Russian Federation's arrangements, although of a markedly different kind, also reflect the cultural and linguistic diversity of the country. Depending on their size and on the territories they have historically occupied, ethnic minorities may have their own autonomous republic, region, or district. These divisions provide varying degrees of autonomy in setting local policies and provide a basis for the preservation of the minorities' cultures. Some of these areas were integrated into the Russian Empire centuries ago, after the lands were taken from the Mongols of the Golden Horde, and others resisted occupation even late in the 19th century. It is not uncommon for Russians to constitute a plurality of the population in these areas. The national government consists of the executive branch, led by a nationally elected president and a prime minister (who is appointed by the president); the parliament; and a judicial branch that resolves constitutional matters.

| Type of administrative division | Kray | Oblast | Autonomous oblast | Autonomous okrug | Republic |

Administrative divisions not named on map

Northwest
1. Kaliningrad
2. Kareliya
3. Leningrad
4. Nizhegorod
5. Novgorod
6. Pskov
7. St. Petersburg (Federal City)
8. Vologda

Central
9. Belgorod
10. Bryansk
11. Ivanovo
12. Kaluga
13. Kostroma
14. Kursk
15. Lipetsk
16. Moscow
17. Oryol
18. Ryazan
19. Smolensk
20. Tambov
21. Tula
22. Tver
23. Vladimir
24. Voronezh
25. Yaroslavl

Southern
26. Adygeya
27. Astrakhan
28. Kalmykiya
29. Krasnodar
30. Rostov
31. Volgograd

North Caucasus
32. Chechnya
33. Dagestan
34. Ingushetiya
35. Kabardino-Balkariya
36. Karachayevo-Cherkesiya
37. North Ossetia
38. Stavropol

Volga
39. Bashkortostan
40. Chuvashiya
41. Mariy-El
42. Mordoviya
43. Orenburg
44. Penza
45. Samara
46. Saratov
47. Tatarstan
48. Udmurtiya
49. Ulyanovsk

Urals
50. Chelyabinsk
51. Kurgan
52. Tyumen

Siberia
53. Altay
54. Buryatiya
55. Kemerovo
56. Khakasiya
57. Novosibirsk
58. Omsk
59. Zabaykalye

Far East
60. Yevrey

© 2010 EB, Inc.

Administrative divisions of Russia. Copyright Encyclopædia Britannica; rendering for this edition by Rosen Educational Services

In other systems, federal arrangements are found in conjunction with a large measure of cultural homogeneity. The Constitution of the United States delegates to the federal government certain activities that concern the whole people, such as the conduct of foreign relations and war and the regulation of interstate commerce and foreign trade. Certain other functions are shared between the federal government and the states, and the remainder are reserved for the states. Although these arrangements require two separate bodies of political officers, two judicial systems, and two systems of taxation, they also allow extensive interaction between the federal government and the states. Thus, the election of Congress and the president, the process of amending the Constitution, the levying of taxes, and innumerable other functions necessitate cooperation between the two levels of government and bring them into a tightly interlocking relationship.

SUBNATIONAL POLITICAL SYSTEMS

Although national government is the dominant form of political organization in the modern world, an extraordinary range of political forms exists below the national level—tribal communities, the intimate political associations of villages and towns, the governments of regions and provinces, the complex array of urban and suburban governments, and the great political and administrative systems of the cities and the metropolises. These subnational entities are, in a sense, the basic political communities—the foundation on which all national political systems are built.

TRIBAL COMMUNITIES

The typical organization of humankind in its early history was the tribe. Today, in many parts of the world, the tribal community is still a major form of human political organization. Even within more formal political systems, traces can still be found of its influence. Some of the *Länder* of modern Germany, such as Bavaria, Saxony, or Westphalia, have maintained their identity since the days of the Germanic tribal settlements. In England, too, many county boundaries can be explained only by reference to the territorial divisions in the period after the end of the Roman occupation.

In many African countries the tribe or ethnic group is still an effective community and a vehicle of political consciousness. (Some African scholars, viewing the term *tribe* as pejorative and inaccurate, prefer to use *ethnic group* or other similar terms to describe such communities.) Most African countries are the successors to the administrative units established by colonial regimes and owe their present boundaries to the often arbitrary decisions of imperial

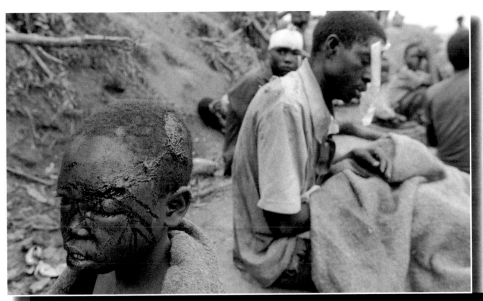

Wounded refugees from the 1994 genocide in Rwanda. Tensions between the country's Hutu and Tutsi tribes resulted in years of political strife and bloodshed. Alexander Joe/AFP/Getty Images

bureaucracies or to the territorial accommodations of rival colonial powers. The result was often the splintering of the tribal communities or their aggregation in largely artificial entities.

Tribal loyalties continue to hamper nation-building efforts in some parts of the world where tribes were once the dominant political structure. Tribes may act through formal political parties like any other interest group. In some cases they simply act out their tribal bias through the machinery of the political system, and in others they function largely outside of formal political structures.

In its primary sense, the tribe is a community organized in terms of kinship, and its subdivisions consist of intimate kindred groupings known as moieties (the two major kinship groups into which a society is organized), gentes (clans), and totem groups (clans or families identified by a common object or emblem). Its territorial basis is rarely defined with any precision, and its institutions are typically undifferentiated and intermittent. The leadership of the tribe is provided by the group of adult males, the lineage elders acting as tribal chiefs, the village headmen, or the shamans (religious functionaries believed to have supernatural powers). These groups and individuals are the guardians of the tribal customs and of an oral tradition of law. Law is thus not made but rather invoked, and its repository is the collective memory of the tribal council or chiefs. This kind of customary law, sanctioned and hallowed by religious belief, nevertheless changes and develops, for each time it is declared something may be added or omitted to meet the needs of the occasion.

VILLAGES AND RURAL COMMUNITIES

The village has traditionally been contrasted with the city: the village is the home of rural occupations and tied to the cycles of agricultural life, while the inhabitants of the city practice many trades, and its economy is founded on commerce and industry. The village is an intimate association of families, while the city is the locus of a mass population. The culture of the village is simple and traditional, while the city is the centre of the arts and sciences and of a complex cultural development. The village and the city offer even sharper contrasts as political communities. Historically, the village has been ruled by the informal democracy of face-to-face discussion in the village council or by a headman whose decisions are supported by village elders or by other cooperative modes of government. Urban government has never been such a simple matter, and monarchical, tyrannical, aristocratic, and oligarchic forms of rule have all flourished in the city. In the village, the boundaries among political, economic, religious, and other forms of action have not been as clearly drawn as in cities.

The origins and development of the apparatus of government can be seen most clearly in the simple political society of the rural community. The transformation of kin-bound societies—with their informal, folk-sustained systems of sociopolitical organization—into differentiated, hierarchical societies with complex political structures began with the enlargement of the rural community. Such enlargement consisted of an increase in the community's population, the diversification of its economy, or interaction with other communities. The rudimentary organs of communal government were then elaborated, the communal functions received more specialized direction, and leadership roles were institutionalized. This was sometimes a process that led by gradual stages to the growth of cities. Elsewhere, however, as in the case of Attica (an east-central district of ancient Greece), the city was established as the result of a process of *synoikismos*, or the uniting of a number of tribal or village communities. This was undoubtedly the origin of Athens, the chief city of Attica. According to its legendary history, Rome also was established as a result of the forcible unification of the tribes that dwelt on the hills surrounding the Palatine Hill.

Even in the nation-states of today's world, the contrasts between the village or the town and the city as centres of human activity are readily apparent. In the country, life is more intimate, human contacts more informal, the structure of society more stable. In the city, the individual becomes anonymous, the contacts between people are mainly formal, and the standing of the individual or the family in society is subject to rapid change. In many contemporary systems, however, the differences in the forms of government of rural and urban communities appear to be growing less pronounced. In the United States, for example, rural institutions have been seriously weakened by the movement of large numbers of people to the city. The township meeting of New England and other forms of direct citizen participation in the affairs of the community have declined in importance and have often been displaced by more formal structures and the growth of local governmental bureaucracies.

CITIES

Cities first emerged as complex forms of social and political organization in the valleys of the Euphrates and Tigris rivers in present-day Iraq, the Nile River in Egypt, and the Huang He (Yellow River) and Yangtze rivers in China. These early cities broke dramatically with the patterns of tribal life and the rural societies from which they sprang. Kinship as the basis of society was replaced by status determined by class and occupation. The animistic or shamanistic leaders of the tribe were displaced by temple priesthoods presiding over highly developed religious institutions and functioning as important agencies of social control. Earlier systems of rule by the tribal chieftains and the simple forms of communal leadership gave way to kingships endowed with magical powers and important religious functions. Specialized functionaries in the royal courts became responsible for supervising new kinds of governmental activity.

Many other developments contributed to the growing centralization of power in these city civilizations. Barter was replaced by more effective systems of exchange, and the wealth generated in commerce and the specialized city trades became both an object of taxation and an instrument of power. Class distinctions emerged as the result of a division of labour and advances in technical development. A military order and a professional soldiery were created and trained in new techniques of warfare, and a slave class provided the work force for large-scale projects of irrigation, fortification, and royal architecture. As these developments proceeded, the city was able to project its power even further into the surrounding countryside, to establish its rule over villages and other cities in its sphere, and finally to become the centre of such early empires as those of Sumeria, Egypt, China, Babylonia, Assyria, and Persia.

A very different form of city life emerged among the Greeks. The Greek polis (city-state) also broke with the folkways of tribal society, but its political development was in striking contrast to the despotism of the East Asian city empires and their massive concentrations of power in the hands of king and priest. As the polis transcended its origins in village life, the powers of the tribal chief dwindled and passed into the hands of aristocratic families. The kingship of Homeric tradition vanished. The "kings" who remained became mere dignitaries in the religious and ceremonial life of the city, and new magistracies and other civic offices were founded. These offices became the focus of factional struggle among the aristocratic families and later, with the weakening of aristocratic rule, the chief prizes in a contest of power between the nobility and the common citizens. Eventually, these developments issued in the characteristic form of Greek city government. A citizen body, always a much narrower group than the total population but often as numerous as the population of freeborn males, acquired power in the direction of the city government through the election of its officers and direct participation in the city councils. Although often interrupted by episodes of oligarchic or tyrannical rule and by periods of civic dissension and class rivalry, the main theme of governmental development in the Greek city was the elaboration of structures that permitted the control of political affairs by its citizens.

Autonomous cities also sprang up in Europe in the later Middle Ages. Medieval city life, although differing from that of the polis and coloured by the forms of feudal society, also emphasized the principle of cooperative association. Indeed, for the first time in the history of city civilization, the majority of the inhabitants of the city were free. The development of trades, the growth of commerce, and the mobilization of wealth emancipated the city from its feudal environment, and the merchant and craft guilds became the bases of a new kind of city democracy. In time, the guilds were transformed into closed corporations and became a basis for oligarchic control, and the city's independence was threatened by the rise of the new nation-states. Tempting targets for the ambition of kings, free European cities such as Venice, Genoa, Florence, Milan, Cologne, Amsterdam, Hamburg, and others eventually succumbed to monarchical control. Theirs was an important legacy, however, because the political order of the medieval city powerfully influenced the development of the constitutional structures of the modern democratic state.

Although cities are generally no longer independent (among the few exceptions are Singapore and Vatican City), the almost universal increase in urban population has made them more important than ever before as centres of human activity. The political organization of modern cities differs from country to country. Even within the same nation-state, there are often important contrasts in the structures of city government. In the United States, for example, three principal types of city government are usually distinguished: the council-manager form, the mayor-council form, and the commission form.

An aerial view of Vatican City, seat of the Roman Catholic Church and the world's smallest independent nation-state. Shutterstock.com

Many American cities with populations over 10,000 operate under council-manager governments. In council-manager systems the council is generally small, being elected at large on a nonpartisan ballot for overlapping four-year terms. No other offices are directly elected, and the mayor, who presides at council meetings and performs mainly ceremonial functions, is chosen by the council from among its members. The manager, a professional city administrator, is selected by the council, serves at the council's pleasure, and is responsible for supervising the city departments and municipal programs, preparing the budget, and controlling expenditures.

Mayor-council governments are found in two basic forms, the "weak" mayor and the "strong" mayor. The former was typical of the 19th-century municipal organization and is now mainly confined to smaller cities. The latter is a common arrangement in cities with significantly larger populations.

In weak-mayor governments, a number of officials, elected or appointed for lengthy terms, wield important administrative powers. The council, typically elected by divisions of the city called wards, is responsible for the direction of the major city agencies, and the mayor's powers of appointment and removal and his control over the city budget are severely limited. In many cases, strong-mayor governments evolved from weak-mayor systems as an independently elected mayor won the power of veto over council ordinances, strengthened his control over appointment and removal, and established himself as the city's chief budgetary officer. At the same time, also, the elective administrative officers and the semi-autonomous appointive boards and commissions were often eliminated and the number of council members reduced.

The commission plan, which has declined in popularity since the early 20th century and is found mainly in smaller cities, concentrates legislative and executive powers in the hands of a small group of commissioners. The commissioners serve individually as the heads of administrative departments and choose one of their number to act as a ceremonial mayor without executive authority.

The variety in the governmental structures of American cities is paralleled in many other countries. Although no longer sovereign, cities are the centres of modern civilization and—both in terms of the services demanded of them and the range and importance of the functions they exercise—the most important of contemporary subnational political systems. Moreover, it is in the cities that most of the problems of modern industrial society seem to have their focus. These problems are not only governmental but also technological, cultural, and economic. They are found in their most acute form in the great metropolitan centres and in that vast urban agglomeration known as the megalopolis. In political terms, the issue that is posed appears to be whether these huge centres of population can continue as effective communities with democratically manageable governments.

REGIONS

In many contemporary national political systems the forces of history and administrative necessity have joined to produce regional communities at an intermediate level between the local and the national community. In some cases—the Swiss canton, the English county, the German *Land*, and the American state—these regional communities possess their own political institutions and exercise governmental functions. In other cases, however, the territorial community is a product of ethnic, cultural, linguistic, physiographic, or economic factors and maintains its identity without the support of political structures.

As subnational political systems, regional communities are sometimes based in tradition, even tracing their origin to a period prior to the founding of the country. In other cases, they are modern administrative units created by national governments for their own purposes. Examples of both types may be found in the history of regionalism in France and its complex pattern of internal territorial divisions. Before the French Revolution, France was divided into ancient provinces—Burgundy, Gascony, Brittany, Normandy, Provence, Anjou, Poitou, and others. After the Revolution, in what seems to have been an effort to discourage regional patriotism and threats of separatism, the Napoleonic government superimposed a new regional structure of *départements* on the old provincial map. More than a century and a half later, in the era of rapid communications and national economic planning, the French national government announced a regrouping of the Napoleonic *départements* into much larger *régions*. Recognizing, perhaps, the continuing strength of the provincial attachments of Gascon, Breton, Norman, and Provençal and the survival of old regional folk cultures with their distinctive patterns of speech, the new *régions* were given boundaries similar in many cases to the traditional provincial boundaries of pre-republican France.

The history of the French regional communities is not a special case, for political, administrative, economic, and technical forces have led many other national governments to replace traditional territorial divisions with new regional units. In England, for example, the traditional structure of county governments was replaced in the late 19th century by a system of administrative counties, many of which in turn lost area to other units of local government in the 1970s and the 1990s. Attempts have also been made to use older regional communities as the infrastructure for new systems of regional government. Thus, the Italian constitution provides for a number of regions, five of which—Valle d'Aosta, Sardinia, Sicily, Trentino–Alto Adige, and Friuli–Venezia Giulia—enjoy a special autonomous status and which, in different ways, are historically distinct from the rest of Italy. In yet other cases the fear of competition from regional governments or of separatist movements has led national governments to make various efforts to resist the development of regional political structures. Again, Italy provides a convenient example, for Italian governments refused to establish all the regions provided for in the 1948 constitution until 1970. It should be noted that the Italian republic of 1870–1922 and its fascist successor state also made similar efforts to combat regional political development—the former by the creation of a large number of administrative provinces and the latter by establishing *corporazione* (corporations or guilds) to represent occupations regardless of geographic location.

In several modern states the growth of vast conurbations (aggregations of urban communities) and the rise of the megalopolis have prompted the development of other kinds of regional governmental structures. The Port of London Authority and the Port Authority of New York and New Jersey are examples of regional systems designed to serve the needs of urban communities that

TENNESSEE VALLEY AUTHORITY

The Tennessee Valley Authority (TVA) is a U.S. government agency established in 1933 to control floods, improve navigation, improve the living standards of farmers, and produce electrical power along the Tennessee River and its tributaries. The Tennessee River was subject to severe periodic flooding, and navigation along the river's middle course was interrupted by a series of shoals at Muscle Shoals, Ala. In 1933 the U.S.

TVA Norris Dam and switching station, Tennessee. Courtesy of the Tennessee Valley Authority

Congress passed a bill establishing the TVA, thus consolidating all the activities of the various government agencies in the area and placing them under the control of a single one. A massive program of building dams, hydroelectric generating stations, and flood-control projects ensued.

The fusion of a broad range of specific powers with a sense of social responsibility to the region made the TVA significant as a prototype of natural-resource planning. Its jurisdiction is generally limited to the drainage basin of the Tennessee River, which covers parts of seven states: Alabama, Georgia, Kentucky, Mississippi, North Carolina, Tennessee, and Virginia. The TVA is a public corporation governed by a board of three directors appointed by the president with the advice and consent of the Senate. The constitutionality of the TVA was immediately challenged upon the agency's establishment, but it was upheld by the Supreme Court in the case of *Ashwander* v. *Tennessee Valley Authority* (1936) and in later decisions.

have outgrown the boundaries of existing city governments. Other regional structures have also resulted from the increased responsibility of national governments for the administration of comprehensive social and economic programs. The Tennessee Valley Authority, for example, is both a national agency and a regional government whose decisions affect the lives of the inhabitants of all the states and cities in its sphere. Further examples of such regional administrative structures include zonal councils established in India for social and economic planning purposes, as well as governmental and economic units established in Britain to deal with the problems of industrially depressed areas.

CHAPTER 2

Types of Government

Confronted by the vast array of political forms, political scientists have attempted to classify and categorize, develop types and models, or in some other way bring analytic order to the bewildering variety of data. Many different schemes have been developed. There is, for example, the classical distinction between governments in terms of the number of rulers—government by one person (monarchy or tyranny), government by the few (aristocracy or oligarchy), and government by the many (democracy). There are schemes classifying governments in terms of their key institutions (for example, parliamentarism, cabinet government, presidentialism). There are classifications that group systems according to basic principles of political authority or the forms of legitimacy (charismatic, traditional, rational-legal, and others). Still other schemes distinguish between different kinds of economic organization in the system (the laissez-faire state, the corporate state, and socialist and communist forms of state economic organization) or between the rule of different economic classes (feudal, bourgeois, and capitalist). Modern efforts compare the functions of political systems, classifying them in terms of structure, function, and political culture.

TYPES OF CLASSIFICATION SCHEME

Although none is comprehensive, each of these principles of analysis has some validity, and the classifying schemes that are based on them—although in some cases no longer relevant to modern forms of political organization—have often been a major influence on the course of political development. The most influential of such classifying schemes is undoubtedly the attempt of Plato and Aristotle to define the basic forms of government in terms of the number of power holders and their use or abuse of power.

Plato held that there was a natural succession of the forms of government. An aristocracy (the ideal form of government by the few) that abuses its power develops into a timocracy (in which the rule of the best persons, who value wisdom as the highest political good, is succeeded by the rule of those who are primarily concerned with honour and martial virtue). Through greed, a timocracy develops into an oligarchy (the perverted form of government by the few), which in turn is succeeded by a democracy. Through excess, a democracy becomes an anarchy (a lawless government), to which a tyrant is inevitably the successor. Abuse of power in the Platonic typology is defined by the rulers' neglect or rejection of the prevailing law or custom (*nomos*). The ideal forms are thus *nomos* observing (*ennomon*), and the perverted forms are *nomos* neglecting (*paranomon*).

Although disputing the character of this implacable succession of the forms of government, Aristotle also based his classification on the number of rulers and distinguished between good and bad forms of government. In his typology it was the rulers' concern for the common good that distinguished the ideal from perverted forms of government. The ideal forms in the Aristotelian scheme are monarchy, aristocracy, and "polity" (a term conveying some of the meaning of the modern concept of constitutional democracy). When perverted by the selfish abuse of power, they are transformed respectively into tyranny, oligarchy, and "ochlocracy" (the mob rule of lawless democracy). The concept of the polity, a mixed or blended constitutional order, fascinated political theorists of subsequent ages. To achieve its advantages, innumerable writers, from Polybius in the 2nd century BCE to St. Thomas Aquinas in the 13th century CE, experimented with the construction of models giving to each social class the control of appropriate institutions of government.

Portrait of the Greek philosopher Aristotle, whose classification of the different forms of government was influential for nearly two millennia. © Photos.com/Getty Images

Another very influential classifying scheme was the distinction between monarchies and republics. In the writings of Niccolò Machiavelli and others, the tripartism of ancient classifications was replaced by the dichotomy of princely and republican rule. Sovereignty in the monarchy or the principality is in the hands of a single ruler, while in republics it is vested in a plurality or collectivity of power holders. Reducing aristocracy and democracy to the single category of republican rule, the Renaissance political theorist Machiavelli also laid the basis in his analysis of the exercise of princely power for a further distinction between despotic and nondespotic forms of government. In the work of the 18th-century political philosopher Montesquieu, for example, despotism, or the lawless exercise of power by the single ruler, is contrasted with the constitutional forms of government of the monarchy and the republic. As a result of the decline of monarchies and the subsequent rise of totalitarian states calling themselves republics, this traditional classification became of little more than historical interest.

MODERN CLASSIFYING SYSTEMS

The usefulness of all the traditional classifications has been undermined by the momentous changes in the political organization of the modern world. Classifications based on the number of power holders or the formal structures of the state are rendered almost meaningless by the standardization of "democratic" forms, the deceptive similarities in the constitutional claims and governmental institutions of regimes that actually differ markedly in their political practices, and the rise of new political orders in the non-Western world.

A number of modern writers have attempted to overcome this difficulty by constructing classifying schemes that give primary importance to social, cultural, economic, or psychological factors. The most influential of such schemes was the Marxist typology, which classified types of rule on the basis of economic class divisions and defined the ruling class as that which controls the means of production in the state. A monistic classification that also emphasized the importance of a ruling class was developed by an Italian theorist of the early 20th century, Gaetano Mosca. In Mosca's writings all forms of government appear as mere facades for oligarchy or the rule of a political elite that centres power in its own hands. Another classification, which distinguishes between "legitimate" and "revolutionary" governments, was suggested by Mosca's contemporary Guglielmo Ferrero. According to Ferrero, a legitimate government is one whose citizens voluntarily accept its rule and freely give it their loyalty, and a revolutionary government is one that fears the people and is feared by them.

Legitimacy and leadership are also the basis of a classification developed by the German sociologist Max Weber. In his scheme there are three basic types of rule: (1) charismatic, in which the authority or legitimacy of the ruler rests upon some genuine sense of calling and in which the followers submit because of their faith or conviction in the ruler's exemplary character, (2) traditional, in which, as in hereditary monarchy, leadership authority is historically or traditionally accepted, and (3) rational-legal, in which leadership authority is the outgrowth of a legal order that has been effectively rationalized and where there is a prevailing belief in the legality of normative rules or commands. The Weberian classification has been elaborated by a number of writers who have found it particularly useful for comparing and classifying the political orders of the non-Western world.

Social scientist Max Weber devised a political classification scheme based on legitimacy and leadership. The Bridgeman Art Library/Getty Images

GAETANO MOSCA

(b. April 1, 1858, Palermo, Sicily, Kingdom of the Two Sicilies [now in Italy]—d. Nov. 8, 1941, Rome, Italy)

Gaetano Mosca was an Italian jurist and political theorist who, by applying a historical method to political ideas and institutions, elaborated the concept of a ruling minority (*classe politica*) present in all societies. His theory seemed to have its greatest influence on apologists for fascism, who misunderstood his view. His work, along with that of Vilfredo Pareto and Robert Michels, inspired subsequent studies by political scientists of the process of the "circulation of elites" within democracies and other political systems.

Educated at the University of Palermo, Mosca taught constitutional law there (1885–88) and at the Universities of Rome (1888–96) and Turin (1896–1908). A member of the Italian Chamber of Deputies beginning in 1908, he served as undersecretary of state for the colonies from 1914 to 1916 and was made a senator for life by King Victor Emmanuel III in 1919. His final speech in the Senate was an attack on the Italian fascist leader Benito Mussolini.

Mosca's *Sulla teorica dei governi e sul governo parlamentare* (1884; "Theory of Governments and Parliamentary Government") was followed by *The Ruling Class* (originally published in Italian, 1896). In these and other writings, but especially in *The Ruling Class*, he asserted—contrary to theories of majority rule—that societies are necessarily governed by minorities: by military, priestly, or hereditary oligarchies or by aristocracies of wealth or of merit. He showed an impartial indifference to the most diverse political philosophies. For him the will of God, the will of the people, the sovereign will of the state, and the dictatorship of the proletariat were all mythical.

Although sometimes called "Machiavellian," Mosca actually considered most of the political ideas of Niccolò Machiavelli

(1469–1527) impractical. He opposed the racist elitism preached by the Nazi Party in Germany, condemned Marxism, which in his view expressed the hatred within Karl Marx, and mistrusted democracy, seeing the greatest threat to liberal institutions in "the extension of the suffrage to the most uncultured strata of the population." Mosca viewed the most enduring social organization as a mixed government (partly autocratic, partly liberal) in which "the aristocratic tendency is tempered by a gradual but continuous renewal of the ruling class" by the addition of individuals of lower socioeconomic origin who have the will and the ability to rule.

A serviceable classification of political systems must penetrate beneath formal appearances to underlying realities. These realities, however, do not consist only of the facts of social and economic organization. Important differences often exist between political systems having very similar socioeconomic structures. That is why some sociological classifications and schemes of analysis fail as tools of political inquiry: they cannot effectively distinguish between certain societies whose political orders are full of contrasts. The political system itself must be the primary focus of inquiry and the phenomena of politics the principal facts of investigation. Such an approach may involve many different kinds of analysis, but it must begin with an examination of the ways in which power is acquired, transferred, exercised, and controlled. This is important for comparing advanced political orders and also for drawing important distinctions between regimes in the underdeveloped areas of the world.

CLASSIFICATION BY MODE OF SUCCESSION

A key problem of all political orders is that of succession. "The king is dead; long live the king" was the answer (not always uncontested) of European hereditary monarchy to the question of who should rule after the death of the king. A second, closely related problem is in what manner and by whom a present ruler may be replaced or deprived of power. To this second question hereditary monarchy gave no definite answer, although the concept of *diffidatio*, or the severance of the bond of allegiance between king and feudal lord, was invoked more than once in the medieval period.

Political systems, even those of tribal societies, have approached both problems in a variety of ways. Anthropological records show that tribal chiefs or kings were sometimes selected as a result of ritual tests or the display of magical signs and proofs of divine origin, usually as determined by the tribal elders or magical leaders. In other cases, a principle of heredity, often diluted by a choice among heirs in terms of physique or warrior ability, was applied. In still other cases, the chief was elected, often from among the adult males of a select group of families.

Techniques for the removal of tribal rulers were equally varied. Sometimes the ruler would be killed after a specified period, or when his magical powers weakened or his physical prowess or health failed. In other cases the chief was exposed to periodic tests of his magical powers or required to accept combat challenges from other qualified candidates for rule. In still other cases the elders could remove him from office.

Techniques for assuring the succession are also varied in the modern world. Succession procedures range from the complex traditional Tibetan process of identifying a

44

reincarnated Dalai Lama to the subtle informal procedures by which parliamentary majorities choose a successor to the office of prime minister in Britain. In fact, however, the succession practices of modern political systems appear to be of four main types: (1) heredity, (2) constitutional prescription, (3) election, and (4) force.

HEREDITARY SUCCESSION

Although dictators still occasionally seek to establish their sons as their heirs, they usually rely on force rather than the claims of heredity to achieve their object. Apart from a few states where the dynastic ruler is the effective head of the government, the hereditary principle of succession is now almost exclusively confined to the constitutional monarchies of western Europe. There is some irony in the fact that the line of succession is more securely established in these monarchies now than at any point in their earlier history. Struggles within dynasties, it appears, are much

ACT OF SETTLEMENT

Since its adoption by Parliament on June 12, 1701, the Act of Settlement has regulated the succession to the throne of Great Britain. Toward the end of 1700, King William III was ill and childless, and his sister-in-law Anne, the prospective queen, had just lost her only surviving child. Abroad, the supporters of the exiled King James II were numerous and active. The need for the act was obvious. It decreed that, in default of issue to either William or Anne, the crown was to pass to Sophia, electress of Hanover and granddaughter of James I, and to "the heirs of her body being Protestants." The act was thus responsible for the accession of Sophia's son George I in 1714—notwithstanding the claims of 57 people closer by the rules of inheritance than Sophia and George. The act also contained a number of constitutional provisions, some of which were subsequently repealed.

less likely when monarchy is mainly ceremonial. Heredity may be reinforced or modified by constitutional prescription, as in the famous Act of Settlement that secured the Hanoverian succession in Britain.

SUCCESSION BY CONSTITUTIONAL PRESCRIPTION

A leading example of succession by constitutional prescription is the United States. Article II, Section 1, of the Constitution of the U.S. provides:

> *In case of the removal of the President from office, or of his death, resignation, or inability to discharge the powers and duties of the said office, the same shall devolve on the Vice President, and the Congress may by law provide for the case of removal, death, resignation, or inability, both of the President and Vice President, declaring what officer shall then act as President, and such officer shall act accordingly, until the disability be removed, or a President shall be elected.*

The Twenty-fifth Amendment to the Constitution, ratified in 1967, elaborated these procedures to include further arrangements for dealing with the problem of presidential disability, as well as for filling a vacant vice presidency. The original language of the Constitution has been the basis for the peaceful succession of Vice Presidents John Tyler, Millard Fillmore, Andrew Johnson, Chester A. Arthur, Theodore Roosevelt, Calvin Coolidge, Harry S. Truman, and Lyndon B. Johnson. Gerald R. Ford succeeded to the presidency on the basis of the provisions of the Twenty-fifth Amendment.

Constitutionally prescribed arrangements for ensuring the succession are not always so successful, however. Many countries whose constitutions contain very similar

Lyndon Johnson taking the oath of office after the assassination of Pres. John F. Kennedy in Dallas, 1963. The Twenty-fifth Amendment provides for the succession of the vice president to the presidency under certain circumstances. National Archives/Getty Images

provisions have experienced succession crises that were resolved only by violence.

SUCCESSION BY ELECTION

Election is a principle of succession also frequently combined with force. In cases of closely contested elections or where there is doubt as to the validity or proper form of the election, the result is often a disputed succession. The Great Schism in the papacy in the 14th century and the disputed succession to the elective kingship of Hungary in the 16th century are examples of the failure of elective systems to assure an orderly succession. Force is the effective basis of succession in several contemporary states in which electoral confirmation is given as a formality to a ruler who seizes power.

The problem of succession imposes great strains on any political order; the continuity of rule is broken, established patterns of action are interrupted, and the future suddenly becomes uncertain. This political crisis tests the character of regimes in ways that are of some importance for comparative political analysis. A number of interesting comparisons may be drawn from the study of succession practices, but perhaps the most important is the distinction between those systems in which the problem is resolved primarily by force and those systems in which heredity, constitutional prescription, or election assure a peaceful and orderly succession.

Political orders are subjected to another kind of strain when the rule of their present power holders is challenged and the question arises of depriving them of authority. This is the problem of the transfer of power: whether, in what way, and by whom a present ruler may be displaced. Like succession, it is a recurrent problem in all political systems. As in the case of succession practices, the ways in which political systems respond to the strains involved offer important clues to their character. It is, in a sense, the fundamental political crisis, for all systems are in some way shaken, often violently and sometimes to the point of destruction, by the struggles between established rulers and their rivals.

SUCCESSION BY FORCE

Revolutions, which are the result of the crisis in its most extreme form, involve the overthrow not merely of the government but of the political order itself. Typically, a revolution is preceded by a series of strains within the system. Challenges to the authority of the government mount, and its legitimacy is increasingly questioned. The exercise of power becomes coercive, and the challenge to rule assumes ever more violent forms. Eventually, the struggle comes to a dramatic climax in the destruction of the old order.

The coup d'etat is another form of violent response to the crisis of rule, but it is distinguished from the revolution in that it involves the overthrow only of the government. The political order is not immediately affected, for the coup is managed by an individual or group within the government or within the ruling class. In some cases, however, the coup d'etat is merely a preliminary stage to revolution. Sometimes this happens when the new ruler leads a governmentally imposed revolution: this was the role played by Napoleon I, Napoleon III, Mussolini, and Hitler. At other times, coups are actually prompted by

Soldiers escorting interim Honduran leader Roberto Micheletti (center) from a press conference in 2009. Micheletti assumed power after a coup forced Pres. Manuel Zelaya into exile. Orlando Sierra/AFP/Getty Images

fear of revolution but succeed only in further weakening the claims to legitimacy of the existing order. In addition to revolutions and coups d'etat, the crisis of rule may prompt other forms of violent political reaction, including civil war and secession, resistance movements and rebellions, guerrilla warfare and terrorism, class warfare, and peasant revolts.

The causes of internal conflict leading to the forcible overthrow of governments are extremely varied. They include: (1) tensions created by rapid social and economic development, (2) the rise of new social classes and the refusal of established elites to share their power, (3) problems of the distribution of wealth and the grievances of different economic groups and interests, (4) the rise of corrosive social and political philosophies and the estrangement of intellectuals, (5) conflict of opinions over the ends of government, (6) factional struggles among power holders or within the ruling class, (7) the rise of a charismatic leader, (8) oppressive rule that alienates powerful groups, and (9) weak rule that tolerates anti-governmental or revolutionary movements. Many other social, economic, and political factors also may play a role. All political systems experience some of these conditions with some frequency. Yet there are a number of modern countries that have avoided internal wars and the forcible overthrow of their governments for considerable periods.

It appears that rulers in the contemporary world are generally safe from violent challenges if they possess an effective monopoly of military, economic, and political power that is linked with certain important social controls. Alternatively, they may be obliged to exercise limited powers for specified periods and be required to yield office to rivals who meet certain qualifications. The first is the definition of a modern totalitarian regime, fully and efficiently organized, and the second describes the governments of several contemporary constitutional democracies. In the first case, the government secures itself by force combined with social and psychological means of preventing the formation of opposition. In the second case, alternatives to internal war are provided by the opportunities for oppositions to influence the exercise of power and ultimately to replace the government. The great achievement of constitutional democracy has been to give reasonable security to governments from forcible overthrow by compelling them to accept limitations on their power, by requiring them to forgo the use of force against rivals who agree to accept the same limitations, and by establishing well-known legal procedures through which these rivals may themselves constitute the government.

AUTOCRATIC VERSUS NONAUTOCRATIC RULE

The preceding discussion has suggested a distinction among political systems in terms of the role played by force in the acquisition and transfer of power. The role of force is vital, also, in distinguishing among political systems in terms of the exercise and control of power. Here the contrast is essentially between "autocratic" and "nonautocratic" governments.

Autocracy is characterized by the concentration of power in a single centre, be it an individual dictator or a group of power holders such as a committee or a party leadership. This centre relies on force to suppress opposition and to limit social developments that might eventuate in opposition. The power of the centre is not subject to effective controls or limited by genuine sanctions; it is absolute power. In contrast, nonautocratic government is characterized by the existence of several centres, each of which shares in the exercise of power. Nonautocratic rule allows the development of social forces that generate a variety of interests and opinions. It also subjects the power holders to reciprocal controls and to effective sanctions of law.

In appearance, autocracy may sometimes be difficult to distinguish from nonautocratic rule. Often, autocracies attempt to borrow legitimacy by adopting the language of the constitutions of nonautocratic regimes or by establishing similar institutions. It is a common practice, for example, in many modern totalitarian states to establish institutions—parliaments or assemblies, elections and parties, courts and legal codes—that differ little in appearance from the institutional structures of constitutional democracies.

Similarly, the language of totalitarian constitutions is often couched in terms of the doctrines of popular rule or democracy. The difference is that in totalitarian regimes neither the institutions nor the constitutional provisions act as effective checks on the power of the single centre: they are essentially facades for the exercise of power through hierarchical procedures that subject all the officials of the state to the commands of the ruling individual or group. The underlying realities of autocratic rule are always the concentration of power in a single centre and the mobilization of force to prevent the emergence of opposition.

Totalitarianism, as already noted, has been a chief form of autocratic rule. It is distinguished from previous forms in its use of state power to impose an official ideology on its citizens. Nonconformity of opinion is treated as the equivalent of resistance or opposition to the government, and a formidable apparatus of compulsion, including various kinds of state police or secret police, is used to enforce the orthodoxy of the proclaimed doctrines of the state. A single party, centrally directed and composed exclusively of loyal supporters of the regime, is the other typical feature of totalitarianism. The party is at once an instrument of social control, a vehicle for ideological indoctrination, and the body from which the ruling group recruits its members.

In the modern world, constitutional democracy is the chief type of nonautocratic government. In institutional terms, the minimal definition of a constitutional democracy is that it should provide for: (1) a regularized system of periodic elections with a free choice of candidates, (2) the opportunity to organize competing political parties, (3) adult suffrage, (4) decisions by majority vote with protection of minority rights, (5) an independent judiciary, (6) constitutional safeguards for basic civil liberties, and (7) the opportunity to change any aspect of the governmental system through agreed procedures.

Two features of constitutional democracy require emphasis in contrasting it with modern totalitarian government: the constitution, or basic law, and the political party. A constitution, as the example of British constitutional democracy suggests, need not be a single written instrument. Indeed, the essence of a constitution is that it formalizes a set of fundamental norms governing the political community and determining the relations between the rulers and the people and the interaction among the centres of power. In most modern constitutional democracies, however, there is a constitutional document providing for fixed limitations on the exercise of power. These provisions usually include three major elements: (1) an assignment of certain specified state functions to different state organs or offices, the delimitation of the powers of each organ or office, and the establishment of arrangements for their cooperative interaction, (2) a list of individual rights or liberties that are protected against the exercise of state power, and (3) a statement of the methods by which the constitution may be amended. With these provisions a concentration of power in the hands of a single ruler is prevented, certain areas of political and social life are made immune to governmental intervention, and peaceable change in the political order is made possible.

The political party is the other chief instrument of constitutional democracy, for it is the agency through which the electorate is involved in both the exercise and transfer of power. In contrast with the centralized, autocratic direction of the totalitarian single-party organization, with its emphasis on ideological conformity and restricted membership, the political parties of constitutional democracy are decentralized, concerned with the integration of many interests and beliefs, and open to public participation. In constitutional democracies there is usually some measure of competition among two or more parties, each of which, if it cannot hope to form a future government, has some ability to influence the course of state action. The party in a constitutional democracy is at once a means of representing a mass electorate in the exercise of power and also a device for allowing the peaceful replacement of one set of power holders with another.

The distinction between autocratic and nonautocratic rule should not conceal the existence of intermediate types that combine elements of both. In these cases, also, the best procedure for comparative purposes is to investigate the power configurations underlying the formal structures and to examine the extent to which power is concentrated in a single centre or the role that is played by force in the maintenance of the regime. It is a type of analysis that, by guiding attention to the relative weight of coercive and consensual power and the scope of individual freedom in the political order, allows comparisons between systems in terms of their most important attributes.

CLASSIFICATION BY STAGE OF DEVELOPMENT

Political life is shaped by a wide variety of factors, including social and cultural conditions, economic organization, intellectual and philosophical influences, geography or climate, and historical circumstance. Recurrent attempts have been made to reduce this range of variables to analytically manageable dimensions. This is partly the motive, for example, of Marxist and other efforts to relate specific types of political systems to stages of economic development or particular kinds of socioeconomic organization. Although interesting interrelations between political and economic development have been discovered, such monistic, or single-factor, approaches are inadequate to the task of explaining political change. The problem is not only that there are many factors that should be examined but also that they are found in different combinations from one society to another. All political orders are unique as products of history and creations of the peculiar forces and conditions of their environment.

A second problem that confronts comparative analysis is the difficulty of devising measures of political development. The definition of what is modern or what constitutes an advanced or developed political system has troubled many writers. Clearly, the older notions of development toward the goals of constitutionalism or democracy must now be seriously questioned, and to judge the maturity of a political system in terms of the extent to which it adopts any particular set of institutions or techniques of rule is an equally doubtful procedure.

Another difficulty is that political change is not simply a reaction to "objective" factors such as economic forces but also the product of conscious manipulation. In explaining the growth and development of political systems it is impossible to ignore the fact that people themselves, having considered the advantages and disadvantages of different forms of government, often decide to adopt one form rather than another. A similar problem arises from the fact that the nature of the interaction between political systems and their environment is extremely complex. For example, to treat the political system as merely the outgrowth of particular patterns of social or economic organization is to ignore the fact that changes in social and economic structures are often the product, sometimes the intended product, of governmental action.

THE EMERGENCE OF ADVANCED NATION-STATES

These difficulties of analysis have prevented the emergence of any satisfactory theory to explain the processes of political change or growth. In the absence of such a theory, however, several writers have attempted to identify certain basic phases in the development of national political systems. For example, five major steps in the emergence of the advanced nation-states of the modern world are often distinguished: (1) unification and independence or autonomy, (2) development and differentiation of political institutions and political roles, (3) transfer of power from traditional elites, (4) further institutional and political role differentiation accompanied by the development of a number of organized social interests and growth in governmental functions, and (5) use of state power in attempts to guide or control social and economic activity, extensive exploitation of resources as the result of technological development, and full participation in the international political system.

Other writers distinguish among "traditional," "transitional," and "modern" societies in an effort to identify differences and regularities in social, economic, cultural, and political development. The social structure of the

traditional society, for example, is described as hierarchical, class bound, based on kinship, and divided into
relatively few effectively organized social groupings. Its
economic basis is primarily agricultural, and industry and
commerce are relatively undeveloped. Its political institutions are those of sacred monarchy, rule by a nobility, and
various forms of particularism.

The social system of the transitional society is typified
by the formation of new classes, especially a middle class
and a proletariat, and conflict among ethnic, religious,
and cultural groupings. Its economic system experiences
major tensions as the result of technological development,
the growth of industry, urbanization, and the use of rapid
communications. Its political institutions are typically
authoritarian, although constitutional forms also make
their appearance.

Modernity is seen as the age of high social mobil-
ity, equality, universal education, mass communications,
increasing secularism, and sociocultural integration. In its
economic system, the modern society experiences a further technological revolution, massive urbanization, and
the development of a fully diversified economy. Its political
institutions are those of democracy and modified totalitarianism, and in either case a specialized bureaucracy is
used to carry on the expanding functions of government.

These efforts to identify stages of "modernization" are
poor substitutes for a general theory of political change, but
they serve to emphasize the increasing complexity of all the
structures—social, economic, and political—of the modern
state. The elaboration of the institutions and procedures of
modern government appears to be partly a reflection of the
social and economic forces at work in the contemporary
world and partly the result of efforts to control these forces
through governmental action. The complex structures of
advanced political orders are treated in the next chapter.

CHAPTER 3

Structures of Government

The study of governmental structures must be approached with great caution, for political systems having the same kind of legal arrangements and using the same type of governmental machinery often function very differently. A parliament, for example, may be an important and effective part of a political system, or it may be no more than an institutional facade of little practical significance. A constitution may provide the framework within which the political life of a state is conducted, or it may be no more than a piece of paper, its provisions bearing almost no relationship to the facts of political life. Political systems must never be classified in terms of their legal structures alone. The fact that two states have similar constitutions with similar institutional provisions and legal requirements should never, by itself, lead to the conclusion that they represent the same type of political system.

To be useful, the study of governmental structures must always proceed hand-in-hand with an investigation of the actual facts of the political process. The analyst must exercise the greatest care in distinguishing between form and reality, between prescription and practice. Approached in this way, an examination of the organizational arrangements that governments use for making decisions and exercising power can be a valuable tool of political inquiry.

CONTEMPORARY FORMS OF GOVERNMENT

Few states in the modern world have constitutional arrangements that are more than a century old. Indeed, the vast majority of all the world's states have constitutions written in the 20th or 21st century. This is true of states that were defeated in World War II, such as Germany, Italy, and Japan, and of other states that experienced civil war and revolutions in the course of the last century, such as the successor states of the Soviet Union, Spain, and China. The United Kingdom and the United States are almost alone among major contemporary nation-states in possessing constitutional arrangements that predate the 20th century.

Even in Britain and the United States, the 20th century saw much change in the governmental system. In the United States, for example, the relationship of legislature and executive at both the national and the state levels was significantly altered by the growth of bureaucracies and the enlargement of the executive's budgetary powers. In Britain, even more far-reaching changes occurred in the

We the People

of the United States, in Order to form a more perfect Union, establish Justice, insure domestic Tranquility, provide for the common defence, promote the general Welfare, and secure the Blessings of Liberty to ourselv   Posterity, do ordain and establish this Constitution for the United States of America.

Tourists filing past the preamble to the U.S. Constitution, writ large on the wall of the National Constitution Center in Philadelphia, Penn., 2003. Pre-20th-century constitutional governments are a rarity. William Thomas Cain/Getty Images

relationship between the prime minister and Parliament and in Parliament's role in supervising the executive establishment. In both countries the appearance of the welfare state, the impact of modern technology on the economy, and international crises resulted in major alterations in the ways in which the institutions of government function and interact.

The modern student of constitutional forms and institutional arrangements confronts an endlessly changing world. In many parts of the world, there have been continuing experiments with new constitutions. The adoption of new constitutions also has been a major aspect of political change in the successor states of the Soviet Union and Yugoslavia. All systems, moreover, even without formal constitutional change, undergo a continual process of adjustment and mutation as their institutional arrangements respond to and reflect changes in the social order and the balance of political forces.

MONARCHY

The ancient distinction among monarchies, tyrannies, oligarchies, and constitutional governments, like other traditional classifications of political systems, is no longer very descriptive of political life. A king may be a ceremonial head of state, as in a parliamentary democracy, or he may be a head of government, perhaps even functioning as an absolute ruler. In the first case his duties may be little different from those of an elected president in many republican parliamentary regimes. In the second his role may be much the same as a dictator in an autocratic regime.

It may be said of the reigning dynasties of modern Europe that they have survived only because they failed to retain or to acquire effective powers of government. Royal lines have been preserved only in those countries

Pres. Barack Obama toasts Queen Elizabeth II during a 2011 state banquet at Buckingham Palace. The queen is England's titular head of state, but the nation's true political power rests outside the monarchy. WPA Pool/Getty Images

of Europe in which royal rule was severely limited prior to the 20th century or in which royal absolutism had never firmly established itself. More successful dynasties, such as the Hohenzollerns in Germany, the Habsburgs in Austria-Hungary, and the Romanovs in Russia, which continued to rule as well as to reign at the opening of the 20th century, paid with the loss of their thrones. Today in countries such as Great Britain, the Netherlands, or Denmark, the monarch is the ceremonial head of state, an indispensable figure in all great official occasions and a symbol of national unity and of the authority of the state. But he is almost entirely lacking in power. Monarchy in the parliamentary democracies of modern Europe has been reduced to the status of a dignified institutional facade behind which the functioning mechanisms of government—cabinet, parliament, ministries, and parties—go about the tasks of ruling.

ROMANOV DYNASTY

The Romanov Dynasty was a royal family that ruled Russia from 1613 until the Russian Revolution of February 1917. The Romanovs acquired their name from Roman Yurev (d. 1543), whose daughter Anastasiya Romanovna Zakharina-Yureva was the first wife of Ivan IV the Terrible (reigned as tsar 1547–84). Her brother Nikita's children took the surname Romanov in honour of their grandfather. After Fyodor I (the last ruler of the Rurik dynasty) died in 1598, Russia endured 15 chaotic years known as the Time of Troubles (1598–1613), which ended when a *zemsky sobor* ("assembly of the land") elected Nikita's grandson, Michael Romanov, as the new tsar.

Royal portrait of Tsar Nicholas II and his family. Popperfoto/Getty Images

The Romanovs established no regular pattern of succession until 1797. During the first century of their rule they generally followed the custom (held over from the late Rurik rulers) of passing the throne to the tsar's eldest son or, if he had no son, to his closest senior male relative. Peter I, who shared power with his half brother Ivan V and became sole ruler upon Ivan's death in 1696, formulated a law of succession (1722) that gave the monarch the right to choose his successor. Peter himself (who was the first tsar to be named emperor) was unable to take advantage of this decree, however, and throughout the 18th century the succession remained vexed.

In 1797, Paul I changed the succession law, establishing a definite order of succession for members of the Romanov family. He was murdered by conspirators supporting his son Alexander I (reigned 1801–25), and the succession following Alexander's death was confused because the rightful heir, Alexander's brother Constantine, secretly declined the throne in favour of another brother, Nicholas I, who ruled from 1825 to 1855. Thereafter the succession followed Paul's rules: Alexander II (1855–81), Alexander III (1881–94), and Nicholas II (1894–1917).

Nicholas II abdicated the throne in favour of his brother Michael, who refused it the following day. Nicholas and all his immediate family were executed in July 1918 at Yekaterinburg.

The 20th century also saw the demise of most of the hereditary monarchies of the non-Western world. Thrones toppled in Turkey, in China, in most of the Arab countries, in the principates of India, in the tribal kingdoms of Africa, and in several countries of Southeast Asia. The monarchs who maintain their position do so less by the claim of legitimate blood descent than by their appeal as popular leaders responsible for well-publicized programs of national economic and social reform or as national military chieftains. In a sense, these kings are less monarchs than monocrats (heads of one-person governments), and their regimes are little different from several other forms of one-person rule found in the modern world.

DICTATORSHIP

While royal rule, as legitimized by blood descent, had almost vanished as an effective principle of government in the modern world, monocracy, or one-person rule—a term that comprehends the rule of non-Western royal absolutists, of generals and strongmen in Latin America and Asia, of a number of leaders in postcolonial Africa, and of the heads of totalitarian communist states—still flourished. Indeed, the 20th century, which witnessed the careers of Kemal Atatürk, Benito Mussolini, Adolf Hitler, Joseph Stalin, Francisco Franco, Mao Tse-tung, Juan Perón, Tito, Gamal Abdel Nasser, Sukarno, Kwame Nkrumah, and Charles de Gaulle, could appear in history as the age of plebiscitary dictatorship.

In many of the states of Africa and Asia, for example, dictators quickly established themselves on the ruins of constitutional arrangements inherited from Western colonial powers. In some of these countries, presidents and prime ministers captured personal power by banning opposition parties and building replicas of the one-party systems of the communist world. In other new countries, the armies seized power, and military dictatorships were established. Whether as presidential dictatorships or as military dictatorships, the regimes that came into being appear to have had common roots in the social and economic problems of the new state. The constitutional systems inherited from the colonial powers proved unworkable in the absence of a strong middle class, and local traditions of autocratic rule retained a powerful

Adolf Hitler (right) with Benito Mussolini. Photos.com/Jupiterimages

influence. The army, one of the few organized forces in society, was also often the only force capable of maintaining order. At the same time, a tiny intellectual class was impatient for economic progress, frustrated by the lack of opportunity, and deeply influenced by the example of authoritarianism in other countries. The dictatorships that resulted proved highly unstable, and few of the individual dictators were able to satisfy for long the demands of the different groups that supported their bids for power.

Although similar in some respects to the dictatorships of the new countries, the caudillos of 19th- and 20th-century Latin America represented a very different type of monocratic rule. In its 19th-century form, caudillismo was the result of the breakdown of central authority. After a brief period of constitutional rule, each of the former Spanish colonies in the Americas experienced a collapse of effective national government. A self-proclaimed leader, usually an army officer, heading a private army typically formed from the peasantry with the support of provincial landowners, established his control over one or more provinces, and then marched upon the national capital. The famous 19th-century caudillos—Antonio López de Santa Anna of Mexico or Juan Manuel de Rosas of Argentina, for example—were thus essentially provincial leaders who seized control of the national government to maintain the social and economic power of provincial groups.

The 20th-century dictatorships in Latin American countries had different aims. The modern caudillo proved to be less a provincial leader than a national one. The Perón regime in Argentina, for example, was established by nationalistic army officers committed to a program of national reform and ideological goals. Often, too, 20th-century dictators in Latin America allied themselves with a particular social class, attempting either to maintain the interests of established economic groupings or to press social reforms.

Dictatorship in the technologically advanced, totalitarian regimes of modern communism was distinctively different from the authoritarian regimes of either Latin America or the postcolonial states of Africa and Asia. Nazi Germany under Hitler and the Soviet Union under Stalin are the leading examples of modern totalitarian dictatorships. The crucial elements of both were the identification of the state with the single mass party and of the party with its charismatic leader, the use of an official ideology to legitimize and maintain the regime, the employment of a terroristic police force and a controlled press, and the application of all the means of modern science and technology to control the economy and individual behaviour. The two systems, however, may be distinguished in several ways. Fascism, in its National Socialist form, was primarily a counterrevolutionary movement that mobilized middle- and lower middle-class groups to pursue nationalistic and militaristic goals and whose sole principle of organization was obedience to the Führer. By contrast, Soviet communism grew out of a revolutionary theory of society, pursued the goal of revolutionary overthrow of capitalist systems internationally, and employed the complex bureaucratic structures of the Communist Party as mechanisms of governmental organization.

Western constitutional democracies have provided examples of another type of contemporary dictatorship. At various points in the 20th and 21st centuries, during periods of domestic or foreign crisis, most constitutional regimes conferred emergency powers on the executive, suspending constitutional guarantees of individual rights or liberties or declaring some form of martial law. Indeed, the constitutions of some Western democracies explicitly provide for the grant of emergency powers to the executive in a time of crisis to protect the constitutional order. In many cases, of course, such provisions have been the instruments with which dictators have overthrown the regime. Thus, the proclamation of emergency rule was the beginning of the dictatorships of Mussolini in Italy, of Kemal Atatürk in Turkey, of Józef Piłsudski in Poland, of António de Olveira Salazar in Portugal, of Franz von Papen and Hitler in Germany, and of Engelbert Dollfuss and Kurt von Schuschnigg in Austria.

In other democracies, however, constitutional arrangements have survived quite lengthy periods of crisis government. After World War II, for example, in both the United States and Britain, the use of extraordinary powers by the executive came to a halt with the end of the wartime emergency. Similarly, although the 1958 constitution of the Fifth Republic of France contained far-reaching emergency powers conferred on the president—"when the institutions of the Republic, the independence of the nation, the integrity of its territory or the fulfillment of its international obligations are threatened with immediate and grave danger, and when the regular functioning of the constitutional authority is interrupted"—their implicit threat to the constitutional order has not been realized.

Many forces at work in the late 20th and early 21st centuries have appeared to lend impetus to the rise of monocratic forms of rule. In nearly all political systems, the powers of chief executives have increased in response to the demanding social, economic, and military crises of the age. The complex decisions required of governments in a technological era, the perfectionist impulses of the great bureaucratic structures that have developed in all industrialized societies, and the imperatives of national survival in a world threatened by weapons of mass destruction continue to add to the process of executive aggrandizement. The question for many constitutional regimes is whether the limitation and balance of power that are at the heart of constitutional government can survive the growing enlargement of executive power.

OLIGARCHY

In the Aristotelian classification of government, there were two forms of rule by the few: aristocracy and its debased form, oligarchy. Many of the classical conditions of oligarchic rule were found until the 20th century in those parts of Asia in which governing elites were recruited exclusively from a ruling caste—a hereditary social grouping set apart from the rest of society by religion, kinship, economic status, prestige, and even language. In the contemporary world, in some countries that have not experienced the full impact of industrialization, governing elites are still often recruited from a ruling class—a stratum of society that monopolizes the chief social and economic functions in the system. Such elites have typically exercised power to maintain the economic and political status quo.

The simple forms of oligarchic rule associated with pre-industrial societies are, of course, rapidly disappearing. Industrialization produces new, differentiated elites that replace the small leadership groupings that once controlled social, economic, and political power in the society. The demands of industrialization compel recruitment on the basis of skill, merit, and achievement rather than on the basis of inherited social position and wealth. New forms of oligarchic rule have also made their appearance in many advanced industrial societies. Although governing elites in these societies are no longer recruited from a single class, they are often not subjected to effective restraints on the exercise of their power. Indeed, in some circumstances, the new elites may use their power to convert themselves into a governing class whose interests are protected by every agency of the state.

Oligarchic tendencies of a lesser degree have been detected in all the great bureaucratic structures of advanced political systems. The growing complexity of modern society and its government thrusts ever greater power into the hands of administrators and committees of experts. Even in constitutional regimes, no fully satisfactory answer has been found to the question of how these bureaucratic decision makers can be held accountable and their powers effectively restrained without, at the same time, jeopardizing the efficiency and rationality of the policy-making process.

CONSTITUTIONAL GOVERNMENT

Constitutional government is defined by the existence of a constitution—which may be a legal instrument or merely a set of fixed norms or principles generally accepted as the fundamental law of the polity—that effectively controls the exercise of political power. The essence of constitutionalism is the control of power by its distribution among several state organs or offices in such a way that they are each subjected to reciprocal controls and forced to cooperate in formulating the will of the state.

Although constitutional government in this sense flourished in England and in some other historical systems for a considerable period, it is only recently that it has been associated with forms of mass participation in politics. In England, for example, constitutional government was not harnessed to political democracy until after the Reform Act of 1832 and subsequent 19th-century extensions of the suffrage. In the contemporary world, however, constitutional governments are also generally democracies, and in most cases they are referred to as constitutional democracies or constitutional-democratic systems.

The contemporary political systems that combine constitutionalism and democracy share a common basis in the primacy they accord to the will of the majority of the people as expressed in free elections. In all such systems, political parties are key institutions, for they are the agencies by which majority opinion in a modern mass electorate is mobilized and expressed. Indeed, the history of the political party in its modern form is coincidental with the development of contemporary constitutional-democratic systems. In each case, the transition from the older forms of constitutionalism to modern constitutional democracy was accompanied by the institutionalization of parties and the development of techniques of party competition. The essential functions of political parties in a constitutional democracy are the integration of a multitude of interests, beliefs, and values into one or more programs or proposals for change and the nomination of party members for elective office in the government. In both functions, the party serves as a link between the rulers and the ruled, in the first case by allowing the electorate to register an opinion on policy and in the second by giving the people a chance to choose their rulers. Of course, the centralized, autocratically directed, and ideologically orthodox one-party systems of totalitarian regimes perform neither of these functions.

The two major types of constitutional democracy in the modern world are exemplified by the United States and Great Britain. The United States is the leading example of the presidential system of constitutional democracy, and Britain is the classic example of the parliamentary system (although its system is sometimes referred to as a cabinet system in recognition of the role of the cabinet in the government). The U.S. presidential system is based on the doctrine of separation of powers and distinguishes sharply between the personnel of the legislature and the executive. The British parliamentary system provides for the integration or fusion of legislature and executive. In the U.S. system the separation of legislature and executive is reinforced by their separate election and by the doctrine of

French prime minister François Fillon (left) and President Nicolas Sarkozy shaking hands in Paris, 2011. French democracy endows both positions with governmental power. Eric Feferberg/AFP/ Getty Images

checks and balances that provides constitutional support for routine disagreements between the branches. In the British system the integration of legislature and executive is reinforced by the necessity for their constant agreement, or for a condition of "confidence" between the two, if the normal processes of government are to continue. In the U.S. system reciprocal controls are provided by such devices as the presidential veto of legislation (which may be overridden by a two-thirds majority in Congress), the Senate's role in ratifying treaties and confirming executive appointments, congressional appropriation of funds and the exclusive ability to declare war, and judicial review of legislation. In the British system the major control device is the vote of "no confidence" or the rejection of legislation that is considered vital.

A third type of constitutional democracy is the hybrid presidential-parliamentary system, exemplified by the government of France. In such systems there is both a directly elected president with substantial executive powers and a presidentially appointed prime minister, who must retain majority support in the legislature. If the president's party or coalition also controls a legislative majority, the prime minister is generally a secondary figure, responsible for the day-to-day running of the government. However, the office of prime minister becomes more important when one party or coalition controls the presidency and a rival party or coalition retains majority support in the legislature. During such periods the president generally appoints the leader of the legislative majority as prime minister.

CONTEMPORARY LEVELS OF GOVERNMENT

Most national societies have passed through a stage in their social and political development, usually referred to as feudalism, in which a weak and ineffectively organized national government competes for territorial jurisdiction with local power holders. In medieval England and France, for example, the crown was perennially threatened by the power of the feudal nobles, and a protracted struggle was necessary before the national domain was subjected to full royal control. Elsewhere, innumerable societies continued to experience this kind of feudal conflict between local magnates and the central government well into the modern era. The warlords of 19th- and 20th-century China, for example, were just as much the products of feudal society as the warring barons of 13th-century England and presented the same kind of challenge to the central government's claim to exercise sovereign jurisdiction over the national territory. By the 1970s, feudalism was almost extinct. The social patterns that had formerly supported the power of local landowners were rapidly disappearing, and central governments had generally acquired a near monopoly of communications and military technology, enabling them to project their power into areas once controlled by local rulers.

In nearly all national political systems, central governments are better equipped than ever before to exercise effective jurisdiction over their territories. In much of the developing world, nationalist political movements and a variety of modern economic forces have swept away the traditional structures of local government, and the quasi-autonomous governments of village, tribe, and province have been replaced by centrally directed systems of sub-national administration. Even in the heavily industrialized states of the modern world, there has been an accelerating tendency toward greater centralization of power at the national level. In the United States, for example, the structure of relationships among the governments at the national, state, and local levels has changed in a number of ways to add to the power of the federal government in Washington. Even though the system of national grants-in-aid appears to have been designed as a means of decentralizing administration, the effect has been decidedly centralist, for the conditional character of the grants has allowed the federal government to exercise influence on state policies in fields that were once invulnerable to national intervention.

NATIONAL GOVERNMENT

The nation-state is the dominant type of political system in the contemporary world, and nationalism, or the creed that centres the supreme loyalty of the people upon the nation-state, is the dominating force in international politics. The national ideal triumphed as a result of the wars of the 19th and 20th centuries. The Napoleonic Wars, which spread the doctrines of the French Revolution, unleashed nationalism as a force in Europe and led to the Risorgimento in Italy and the emergence of Bismarck's Germany. The two world wars of the 20th century carried the principles of national self-determination and liberal democracy around the world and gave birth to the independence movements that resulted in the foundation of new states in eastern Europe in 1919 and the emergence from colonial status of countries in Asia and Africa after 1945. The collapse of the Warsaw Pact and the Soviet Union itself completed this process of moving from multinational empires to truly sovereign national states.

All the major forces of world politics—e.g., war, the development of national economies, and the demand for social services—have reinforced the national state as the primary focus of people's loyalties. Wars have played the major part in strengthening national governments and weakening political regionalism and localism. The

RISORGIMENTO

The Risorgimento (Italian: "Rising Again") was a 19th-century movement for Italian unification that culminated in the establishment of the Kingdom of Italy in 1861. It was an ideological and literary movement that helped to arouse the national consciousness of the Italian people, and it led to a series of political events that freed the Italian states from foreign domination and united them politically. Although the Risorgimento has attained the status of a national myth, its essential meaning remains a controversial question. The classic interpretation (expressed in the writings of the philosopher Benedetto Croce) sees the Risorgimento as the triumph of liberalism, but subsequent views criticize it as an aristocratic and bourgeois revolution that failed to include the masses.

The main impetus to the Risorgimento came from reforms introduced by the French when they dominated Italy during the period of the French Revolutionary and Napoleonic wars (1796–1815). A number of Italian states were briefly consolidated, first as republics and then as satellite states of the French empire. Even more importantly, the Italian middle class grew in numbers and was allowed to participate in government.

After Napoleon's defeat in 1815, the Italian states were restored to their former rulers. Under the domination of Austria, these states took on a conservative character. Secret societies such as the Carbonari opposed this development in the 1820s and '30s. The first avowedly republican and national group was Young Italy, founded by Giuseppe Mazzini in 1831. This society, which represented the democratic aspect of the Risorgimento, hoped to educate the Italian people to a sense of their nationhood and to encourage the masses to rise against the existing reactionary regimes. Other groups, such as the Neo-Guelfs, envisioned an Italian confederation headed by the pope. Still others favoured unification under the house of Savoy, which ruled the liberal northern Italian state of Piedmont-Sardinia.

After the failure of liberal and republican revolutions in 1848, leadership passed to Piedmont. With French help, the Piedmontese defeated the Austrians in 1859 and united most of Italy under their rule by 1861. The annexation of Venetia in 1866 and papal Rome in 1870 marked the final unification of Italy and hence the end of the Risorgimento.

attachments that people have to subnational political communities are loosened when they must depend for their security on the national power. Even in the new age of total war—which few countries are capable of waging and even fewer of surviving—people look for their security to national governments rather than to international organizations. In nearly all contemporary states, the national budget is dominated by expenditures for defense, the military employs the largest fraction of the work force, and questions of national security pervade the discussion of politics.

One of the lessons of the last century was that national sovereignty continues to be the most important obstacle not only to the emergence of new forms of supranational government but to effective international cooperation as well. Almost everywhere, attempts to achieve federation and other forms of multinational communication have foundered on the rocks of nationalism. The collapse of the Federation of Rhodesia and Nyasaland and the Federation of Malaya, for example, were paralleled by the seeming ineffectiveness of the Organization of American States and the Arab League. On another level was the collapse of the Warsaw Pact when the countries of eastern Europe reclaimed their sovereignty in the late 1980s after decades of domination by the Soviet Union. In western Europe, however, countries joined together to form the supranational European Communities, which ultimately were succeeded by the European Union (EU) and expanded to encompass the bulk of the European continent. The countries of the EU are united not only by a long history and a common cultural inheritance but also by the expectation of mutual economic advantage. Even in this case, though, nationalism has proved to be an obstacle to the most ambitious goals of unification, which would severely limit national sovereignty in some spheres.

At the international level, anarchy is the principal form of contemporary rule, for the nation-state's freedom of action is limited only by its power. While the state's freedom of action may not be directly threatened, the effectiveness of the state's action in the economic realm is increasingly being called into question. The development of national industries in the 19th and early 20th centuries played a major part in strengthening national as against regional and local political entities, but the scale of economic activity has now outgrown national markets. Industrial combines and commercial groupings have emerged that cross national frontiers and require international markets. This tight integration of the world economy has limited the effectiveness of some traditional instruments used to influence national trends in capitalist economies.

It is increasingly clear that some aspects of traditional sovereignty may be affected by serious efforts to confront some issues that act on the entire international system. National frontiers can no longer be adequately defended in an era of long-range ballistic missiles and international terrorism, especially with the rapid diffusion of the technology of weapons of mass destruction. Action in this area is, by definition, an attempt to shape the national security policy of states, something very near the core of a state's sovereignty. Concern over environmental matters, notably global climate change, could lead to more restrictive regimes than any arms-control provisions, ultimately shaping the way in which countries evolve economically. Destruction of major ecosystems, wasteful use of energy, and industrialization based on the use of fossil fuels are all national policies with international repercussions. Avoiding global economic crises such as the Great Recession of 2008–09 may require countries to coordinate, as well as to increase, their regulation of multinational banks and financial markets. In all of these areas, there are increasing incentives to limit the domestic policy choices of all countries.

REGIONAL AND STATE GOVERNMENT

Montesquieu wrote that governments are likely to be tyrannical if they are responsible for administering large territories, for they must develop the organizational capacity characteristic of despotic states. It was partly this fear that led the American Founding Fathers to provide for a federal system and to divide governmental functions between the government in Washington and the state governments. Modern technology and mass communication are often said to have deprived Montesquieu's axiom of its force. Yet the technology that makes it possible for large areas to be governed democratically also holds out the spectre of an even greater tyranny than Montesquieu foresaw.

In all political systems the relationships between national and regional or state governments have been affected by technology and new means of communication. In the 18th century Thomas Jefferson—in arguing that local government, or the government closest to the people, was best—could claim that citizens knew most about their local governments, somewhat less about their state governments, and least about the national government. In the present-day United States, however, the concentration of the mass media on the issues and personalities of national government has made nonsense of this proposition. As several studies have demonstrated, people know much less about local and state government than national government and turn out to vote in much larger numbers in national elections. The necessity for employing systems for the devolution of political power is reduced when a central government can communicate directly with citizens in all parts of the national territory, and the vitality of subnational levels of government is sapped when public attention is focused on national problems.

Another general development that has lessened the importance of regional or state government is the rise of efficient national bureaucracies. In nearly all political systems, there has been some tendency toward bureaucratic centralization, and in some cases national bureaucracies have almost completely replaced older systems of regional and provincial administration. In the United States, for example, complex programs of social security, income taxes, agricultural subsidies, and many others that bear directly on individuals are centrally administered.

Even in systems in which a division of functions between national and subnational governments is constitutionally prescribed, the prevailing trend in intergovernmental relations is toward increasing involvement of the national government in areas once dominated by regional or state governments. Thus, the original constitutional arrangements prescribed by the Allied powers for the West German republic in 1949 won general acclaim at the time because they provided for greater decentralization than had the Weimar Constitution (1919–33). But, as soon as Germany was free to amend its own constitution, several state functions were reassigned to the national government. In the United States, also, the collapse of the doctrine of "dual federalism," according to which the powers of the national government were restricted by the powers reserved to the states, signalled the end of an era in which the states could claim exclusive jurisdiction over a wide range of functions. Today, forms of cooperative federalism involving joint action by national and state governments are increasingly common. Such cooperative relationships in the United States include programs of public assistance, the interstate highway system, agricultural extension programs, and aid to education. In some areas, such as school desegregation, the national government has used broad powers to compel states to conform to national standards.

Nevertheless, efforts made to reinvigorate regional or state governments have met with some measure of success in countries such as France, Italy, and Belgium. Moreover, popular attempts to reverse the trend toward national centralization have succeeded in regions with historically strong nationalist or separatist movements—for example, in Scotland, Wales, and Northern Ireland, Quebec, and Brittany.

CITY AND LOCAL GOVERNMENT

Political scientists since Aristotle have recognized that the nature of political communities changes when their populations grow larger. One of the central problems of contemporary government is the vast increase in urban population and the progression from "polis to metro-polis to mega-polis." The catalog of ills that have resulted from urban growth includes political and administrative problems of extraordinary complexity.

Aging infrastructure has become an issue of pressing national importance in the United States, with the major cities obviously suffering in this area. Grave social problems—for example, violent crime (especially that committed by youths in poverty-stricken areas), drug trafficking, unemployment, and homelessness—are concentrated to such a degree that they directly shape the environment in many large urban areas. The majority of cities are ill equipped to handle these problems without significant assistance from the national government. Yet, in the latter half of the 20th century, the tax base of many U.S. cities dwindled, with the flight of the middle classes to the suburbs and the relocation of industry. Largely as a result of this trend, political power began to follow wealth out of the cities and into adjoining suburbs, which in turn served to reduce the national government's activism in the cities.

The metropolis suffers from several acute governmental and administrative failures. Responsibility for the issues that transcend the boundaries of local governments has not been defined, for representative institutions have failed to develop at the metropolitan level. In most cases, there are no effective governmental structures for administering area-wide services or for dealing comprehensively with the common problems of the metropolitan community. The result has been the appearance of a new class of problems created by government itself, including uneven levels of service for metropolitan residents, inequities in financing government services and functions, and variations in the democratic responsiveness of the governments scattered through the metropolitan area. The tangled pattern of local governments, each operating in some independent sphere, does not allow the comprehensive planning necessary to deal with the escalating problems of urban life.

Efforts to create new governing structures for metropolitan communities have been among the most interesting developments in contemporary government. In the United States these efforts include the creation of special districts to handle specific functions, area-wide planning agencies, interstate compacts, consolidated school and library systems, and various informal intergovernmental arrangements. Although annexation of outlying areas by the central city and city-county consolidations have been attempted in many cases, the reluctance of urban areas to surrender their political independence or to pay for central-city services has been an obstacle. The Los Angeles plan, by which the county assumed responsibility for many area-wide functions, leaving the local communities with substantial political autonomy, may represent a partial solution to the problem of urban-suburban tensions. In other cases, "metropolitan federation" has been attempted.

One of the earliest and most influential examples of a federated system of metropolitan government is Greater London, which encompasses 33 London boroughs and places effective governing powers in the hands of an elected mayor and assembly. In Canada the city of Toronto and its suburbs adopted a metropolitan "constitution" in 1953 under which mass transit, highways, planning, and several other functions were controlled by a council composed of elected officials from the central city and surrounding governments. Further restructuring and reform of Toronto's government took place in 1998 and 2007. Cities in the United States that have undertaken various degrees of area-wide consolidation include Miami, Nashville, Seattle, and Indianapolis.

Most of the major problems of contemporary politics seem to have found their focus in the metropolis, and there is almost universal agreement that new governing

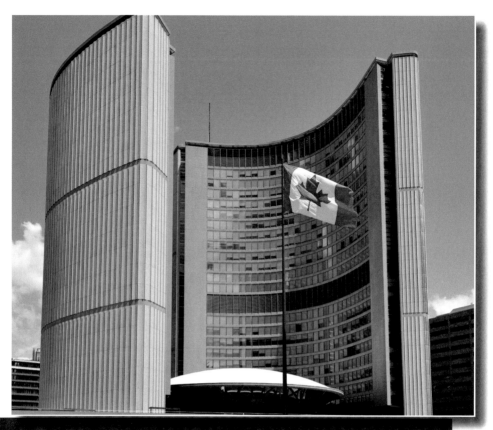

The Canadian flag flying in front of Toronto's city hall in July 2010. From 1953 through 1997, the city of Toronto and five suburbs operated under a municipal government. Zoran Karapancev/ Shutterstock.com

systems must be devised for the metropolitan community if the problems are ever to be resolved.

CONTEMPORARY DIVISIONS OF GOVERNMENT

In his *Politics*, Aristotle differentiated three categories of state activity—deliberations concerning common affairs, decisions of executive magistrates, and judicial rulings— and indicated that the most significant differences among constitutions concerned the arrangements made for these activities. This threefold classification is not precisely the same as the modern distinction between legislature, executive, and judiciary. Aristotle intended to distinguish certain state functions and stopped short of recommending that they be assigned as powers to separate organs of government. Indeed, since Aristotle held that all power should be wielded by one man, pre-eminent in virtue, he never considered the concept of separated powers. In the 17th century the English political philosopher John Locke also distinguished the legislative from the executive function but, like Aristotle, failed to assign these to separate organs or institutions.

Montesquieu was the first to make the modern division between legislative, executive, and judiciary. Arguing that the purpose of political association is liberty, not virtue, and that the very definition of liberty's great antagonist, tyranny, is the accumulation of all power in the same hands, he urged the division of the three functions of government among three separate institutions. After Montesquieu, the concept of separation of powers became one of the principal doctrines of modern constitutionalism. Nearly all modern constitutions, from the document written at Philadelphia in 1787 through the French Declaration of the Rights of Man and of the Citizen of August 1789 up to the constitutions of the postcolonial countries of Africa and Asia, provide for the separate establishment of legislative, executive, and judiciary.

The functional division between the branches of government, however, is never precise. In the American system, for example, the doctrine of checks and balances justifies several departures from the strict assignment of functions to the branches. Parliamentary forms of government depart even further from the concept of separation and integrate both the personnel and the functions of the legislature and the executive. Indeed, the principle of shared rather than separated powers is the true essence of constitutionalism. In the constitutional state, power is controlled because it is shared or distributed in such a way that the divisions of government are each subjected to reciprocal checks and forced to cooperate in the exercise of political power. In the nonconstitutional systems of totalitarianism or autocracy, although there may be separate institutions such as legislatures, executives, and judiciaries, power is not shared but rather concentrated in a single organ. Because this organ is not subjected to the checks of shared power, the exercise of political power is uncontrolled or absolute.

THE EXECUTIVE

Political executives are government officials who participate in the determination and direction of government policy. They include heads of state and government leaders—presidents, prime ministers, premiers, chancellors, and other chief executives—and many secondary figures, such as cabinet members and ministers, councillors, and agency heads. By this definition, there are several thousand political executives in the U.S. national government, including the president; dozens of political appointees in the cabinet departments, in the agencies, in the commissions, and in the White House staff; and hundreds of senior civil servants. The same is true of most advanced political systems, for the making and implementation of government policy require very large executive and administrative establishments.

The crucial element in the organization of a national executive is the role assigned to the chief executive. In presidential systems, such as in the United States, the president is both the political head of the government and also the ceremonial head of state. In parliamentary systems, such as in Great Britain, the prime minister is the national political leader, but another figure, a monarch or elected president, serves as the head of state. In mixed presidential-parliamentary systems, such as that established in France under the constitution of 1958, the president serves as head of state but also wields important political powers, including the appointment of a prime minister and cabinet to serve as the government.

The manner in which the chief executive is elected or selected is often decisive in shaping his role in the political system. Thus, although he receives his seals of office from the monarch, the effective election of a British prime minister usually occurs in a private conclave of the leading members of his party in Parliament. Elected to Parliament from only one of several hundred constituencies, he is tied to the fortunes of the legislative majority that he leads. In contrast, the U.S. president is elected by a nation-wide electorate, and, although he leads his party's ticket, his fortunes are independent of his party. Even when the opposition party controls the Congress, his fixed term and his independent base of power allow him considerable freedom of maneuver. These contrasts explain many of the differences in the roles of the two chief executives. The British prime minister invariably has served for many years in Parliament and has developed skills in debate and in political negotiation. His major political tasks are the designation of the other members of the cabinet, the direction of parliamentary strategy, and the retention of the loyalty of a substantial majority of his legislative party. The presidential chief executive, on the other hand, often lacks prior legislative and even national-governmental experience, and his main concern is with the cultivation of a majority in the electorate through the leadership of public opinion. Of course, since the president must have a legislative program and often cannot depend on the support of a congressional majority, he may also need the skills of a legislative strategist and negotiator.

Another important area of contrast between different national executives concerns their role in executing and administering the law. In the U.S. presidential system, the personnel of the executive branch are constitutionally separated from the personnel of Congress: no executive officeholder may seek election to either house of Congress, and no member of Congress may hold executive office. In parliamentary systems the political management of government ministries is placed in the hands of the party leadership in parliament. In the U.S. system the president often appoints to cabinet positions persons who have had little prior experience in politics, and he may even appoint members of the opposition party. In the British system, cabinet appointments are made to consolidate the prime minister's personal ascendancy within the parliamentary party or to placate its different factions. These differences extend even further into the character of the two systems of administration and the role played by civil servants. In the U.S. system a change in administration is accompanied by the exodus of a very large number of top government executives—the political appointees who play the vital part in shaping day-to-day policy in all the departments and agencies of the national government. In Britain, when political control of the House of Commons changes, only the ministers, their parliamentary secretaries, and one or two other top political aids are replaced. For all practical purposes, the ministries remain intact and continue under the supervision of permanent civil servants.

In nearly all political systems—even in constitutional democracies where executive responsibility is enforced through free elections—the last century saw a remarkable increase in the powers of chief executives. The office of the presidency in the United States, like the office of prime minister in Britain, greatly enlarged the scope of its authority. One of the challenges of representative government is to develop more constitutional restraints on the abuse of executive powers while retaining their advantages for effective rule.

THE LEGISLATURE

The characteristic function of all legislatures is the making of law. In most systems, however, legislatures also have other tasks, such as selection and criticism of the government, supervision of administration, appropriation of funds, ratification of treaties, impeachment of executive and judicial officials, acceptance or refusal of executive nominations, determination of election procedures, and public hearings on petitions. Legislatures, then, are not simply lawmaking bodies. Neither do they monopolize the function of making law. In most systems the executive has a power of veto over legislation, and, even where this is lacking, the executive may exercise original or delegated powers of legislation. Judges, also, often share in the lawmaking process, through the interpretation and application of statutes or, as in the U.S. system, by means of judicial review of legislation. Similarly, administrative officials exercise quasi-legislative powers in making rules and deciding cases that come before administrative tribunals.

Legislatures differ strikingly in their size, the procedures they employ, the role of political parties in legislative action, and their vitality as representative bodies. In size, the British House of Commons, with more than 600 members, is among the largest. In contrast, numerous small island countries have legislative bodies with fewer than 20 members. Bicameral legislatures are common in many countries, particularly those with a federal system of government, such as the United States, Australia, Brazil, Canada, Germany, and India. Unicameral legislatures are typical in small countries and in those with a unitary system of government, such as New Zealand and Denmark. However, a federal system does not necessarily imply a bicameral legislature, nor do all unitary systems have unicameral legislatures.

The procedures of the United States House of Representatives, which derive from a manual of procedure written by Thomas Jefferson, are among the most elaborate of parliamentary rules, requiring study and careful observation over a considerable period before members become proficient in their manipulation. Voting procedures range from the formal procession of the division or teller vote in the British House of Commons to the electric voting methods employed in many U.S. states. Another point of difference among legislatures concerns their presiding officers. These are sometimes officials who stand above party and, like the speaker of the British House of Commons, exercise a neutral function as parliamentary umpires. In some cases they are the leaders of the majority party and, like the speaker of the United States House of Representatives, major political figures. In other cases they are officials who, like the vice president of the United States in his role as presiding officer of the Senate, exercise a vote to break ties and otherwise perform mainly ceremonial functions.

Legislative parties are of various types and play a number of roles or functions. In the United States House of Representatives, for example, the party is responsible for assigning members to all standing committees, the party leadership fills the major parliamentary offices, and the party membership on committees reflects the proportion of seats held by the party in the House as a whole. The congressional party, however, is not disciplined to the degree found in British and some other European legislative parties, and there are relatively few "party line" votes in which all the members of one party vote against all the members of the other party. In the House of Commons, party-line voting is general. Indeed, it is very unusual to find members voting against their party leadership, and, when they do, they must reckon with the possibility of penalties such as the "withdrawal of the whip," or the loss of their official status as party members.

It is often said that the 20th century dealt harshly with legislatures, leading to executive aggrandizement. Certainly, executives in most countries have assumed an increasingly large role in the making of law, through the initiation of the legislation that comes before parliaments, assemblies, and congresses, through the exercise of various rule-making functions, and as a result of the growth of different types of delegated legislation. It is also true that executives have come to predominate in the sphere of foreign affairs and, by such devices as executive agreements, which are frequently used in place of treaties, have freed themselves from dependence upon legislative approval of important foreign-policy initiatives. Moreover, devices such as the executive budget and the rise of specialized budgetary agencies in the executive division have threatened the traditional fiscal controls of legislatures.

This decline in legislative power, however, is not universal. The United States Congress, for example, has preserved a substantial measure of its power. Indeed, congressional oversight of the bureaucracy is an area in which it has added to its power and has developed new techniques for controlling the executive. The difficulties of presidents with legislative programs of foreign aid and the perennial congressional criticism of executive policies in foreign affairs also suggest that Congress continues to play a vital role in the governing process.

THE JUDICIARY

Like legislators and executives, judges are major participants in the policy-making process. Courts, like legislatures and administrative agencies, promulgate rules of behaviour having the nature of law. The process of judicial decision making, or adjudication, is distinctive, however, for it is concerned with specific cases in which an individual has come into conflict with society by violating its norms or in which individuals have come into conflict with one another, and it employs formal procedures that contrast with those of parliamentary or administrative bodies.

Established court systems are found in all advanced political systems. Usually there are two judicial hierarchies, one dealing with civil and the other with criminal cases, each with a large number of local courts, a lesser number at the level of the province or the region, and one or more courts at the national level. This is the pattern of judicial organization in Britain, for example. In some countries—for example, in France—although there is a double hierarchy, the distinction is not between courts dealing with criminal cases and other courts dealing with civil cases but rather between those that handle all civil and criminal cases and those that deal with administrative cases or challenges to the administrative authority of the state. Reflecting the federal organization of its government, the United States has two court systems: one set of national courts and 50 sets of state courts. By contrast, Germany, which is federal in governmental organization, possesses only a single integrated court system.

Local courts are found in all systems and are usually of two types. The first type deals with petty offenses and may include a traffic court, a municipal court, a small-claims court, and a court presided over by a justice of the peace or a local magistrate. The second type, sometimes called trial courts, are courts of first instance in which most cases of major importance are begun. These are the state superior courts in the United States, the county courts and quarter sessions in Britain, the *tribunal de grande instance* in France, and the district courts, or *Landgerichte*, in Germany. In some systems there is a level above the local court, usually referred to as assize courts, in which exceptionally serious crimes, such as homicide, are tried. Courts of appeal review the procedures and the law in the lower court and, in some instances, return the case for a new trial. In all systems there are national supreme courts that hear appeals and exercise original jurisdiction in cases of the greatest importance, such as those involving conflict between a state and a national government. Outside the regular court systems, there are sometimes found specialized judicial tribunals, such as administrative courts, or courts of claims that deal with special categories of cases.

CHAPTER 4

Functions of Government

In all modern states, governmental functions have greatly expanded with the emergence of government as an active force in guiding social and economic development. In countries with a command economy, government has a vast range of responsibilities for many types of economic behaviour. In those countries favouring social democracy, the government owns or regulates business and industry. Even in the capitalist economy of the United States—where there remains a much greater attachment than in most societies to the idea that government should be only an umpire adjudicating the rules by which other forces in society compete—some level of government regulation, such as the use of credit controls to prevent economic fluctuations, is now accepted with relatively little question. Government has thus become the major or even the dominant organizing power in all contemporary societies.

The historical stages by which governments have come to exercise their contemporary functions make an interesting study in themselves. The scope of government in the ancient polis involved the comprehensive regulation of the ends of human existence. As Aristotle expressed it, what was not commanded by government was forbidden. The extent of the functions of government in the ancient world was challenged by Christianity and its insistence on a division of those things that belong separately to Caesar and to God. When the feudal world succeeded the Roman Empire, however, the enforcement of the sanctions of religion became one of the first objects of political authority. The tendencies that began in the 18th century separated church from state and state from society, and the modern concept of government came into being.

The American colonies' Declaration of Independence expresses the classic modern understanding of those ends that governmental functions exist to secure. The first aim of government is to secure the right to life, which comprehends the safety of fellow citizens as regards one another and the self-preservation of the country as regards foreign powers. Life exists for the exercise of liberty, in terms of both natural and civil rights, and these, along with other specific functions of government, provide those conditions upon which people may pursue happiness, an end that is finally entirely private and beyond the competence of government.

With the advent of the Marxist conception of the state, the ends of human existence once again became the objects of comprehensive government regulation. Marxism sees the state as a product of class warfare that will pass out of existence in the future age of perfect freedom. Aristotle believed human perfection to be possible only within political society, while Marx believed that the perfection of humans would follow upon the abolition of political society. Before the final disposal of the state, however, some Marxists believe that forceful use of governmental power is justified in order to hasten humankind's progress toward the last stage of history.

THE TASKS OF GOVERNMENT

The chief tasks of government are self-preservation, the supervision and resolution of conflicts, regulation of the economy, the protection of political and social rights, and the provision of goods and services.

In CONGRESS, July 4, 1776.

A DECLARATION

By the REPRESENTATIVES of the

UNITED STATES OF AMERICA,

In GENERAL CONGRESS ASSEMBLED.

WHEN in the Course of human Events, it becomes necessary for one People to dissolve the Political Bands which have connected them with another, and to assume among the Powers of the Earth, the separate and equal Station to which the Laws of Nature and of Nature's God entitle them, a decent Respect to the Opinions of Mankind requires that they should declare the causes which impel them to the Separation.

We hold these Truths to be self-evident, that all Men are created equal, that they are endowed by their Creator with certain unalienable Rights, that among these are Life, Liberty, and the Pursuit of Happiness—That to secure these Rights, Governments are instituted among Men, deriving their just Powers from the Consent of the Governed, that whenever any Form of Government becomes destructive of these Ends, it is the Right of the People to alter or to abolish it, and to institute new Government, laying its Foundation on such Principles, and organizing its Powers in such Form, as to them shall seem most likely to effect their Safety and Happiness. Prudence, indeed, will dictate that Governments long established should not be changed for light and transient Causes; and accordingly all Experience hath shewn, that Mankind are more disposed to suffer, while Evils are sufferable, than to right themselves by abolishing the Forms to which they are accustomed. But when a long Train of Abuses and Usurpations, pursuing invariably the same Object, evinces a Design to reduce them under absolute Despotism, it is their Right, it is their Duty, to throw off such Government, and to provide new Guards for their future Security. Such has been the patient Sufferance of these Colonies; and such is now the Necessity which constrains them to alter their former Systems of Government. The History of the present King of Great-Britain is a History of repeated Injuries and Usurpations, all having in direct Object the Establishment of an absolute Tyranny over these States. To prove this, let Facts be submitted to a candid World.

He has refused his Assent to Laws, the most wholesome and necessary for the public Good.

He has forbidden his Governors to pass Laws of immediate and pressing Importance, unless suspended in their Operation till his Assent should be obtained; and when so suspended, he has utterly neglected to attend to them.

He has refused to pass other Laws for the Accommodation of large Districts of People, unless those People would relinquish the Right of Representation in the Legislature, a Right inestimable to them, and formidable to Tyrants only.

He has called together Legislative Bodies at Places unusual, uncomfortable, and distant from the Depository of their public Records, for the sole Purpose of fatiguing them into Compliance with his Measures.

He has dissolved Representative Houses repeatedly, for opposing with manly Firmness his Invasions on the Rights of the People.

He has refused for a long Time, after such Dissolutions, to cause others to be elected; whereby the Legislative Powers, incapable of Annihilation, have returned to the People at large for their exercise; the State remaining in the mean time exposed to all the Dangers of Invasion from without, and Convulsions within.

He has endeavoured to prevent the Population of these States; for that Purpose obstructing the Laws for Naturalization of Foreigners; refusing to pass others to encourage their Migrations hither, and raising the Conditions of new Appropriations of Lands.

He has obstructed the Administration of Justice, by refusing his Assent to Laws for establishing Judiciary Powers.

He has made Judges dependent on his Will alone, for the Tenure of their Offices, and the Amount and Payment of their Salaries.

He has erected a Multitude of new Offices, and sent hither Swarms of Officers to harrass our People, and eat out their Substance.

He has kept among us, in Times of Peace, Standing Armies, without the consent of our Legislatures.

He has affected to render the Military independent of and superior to the Civil Power.

He has combined with others to subject us to a Jurisdiction foreign to our Constitution, and unacknowledged by our Laws; giving his Assent to their Acts of pretended Legislation:

For quartering large Bodies of Armed Troops among us:

For protecting them, by a mock Trial, from Punishment for any Murders which they should commit on the Inhabitants of these States:

For cutting off our Trade with all Parts of the World:

For imposing Taxes on us without our Consent:

For depriving us, in many Cases, of the Benefits of Trial by Jury:

For transporting us beyond Seas to be tried for pretended Offences:

For abolishing the free System of English Laws in a neighbouring Province, establishing therein an arbitrary Government, and enlarging its Boundaries, so as to render it at once an Example and fit Instrument for introducing the same absolute Rule into these Colonies:

For taking away our Charters, abolishing our most valuable Laws, and altering fundamentally the Forms of our Governments:

For suspending our own Legislatures, and declaring themselves invested with Power to legislate for us in all Cases whatsoever.

He has abdicated Government here, by declaring us out of his Protection and waging War against us.

He has plundered our Seas, ravaged our Coasts, burnt our Towns, and destroyed the Lives of our People.

He is, at this Time, transporting large Armies of foreign Mercenaries to compleat the Works of Death, Desolation, and Tyranny, already begun with circumstances of Cruelty and Perfidy, scarcely paralleled in the most barbarous Ages, and totally unworthy the Head of a civilized Nation.

He has constrained our fellow Citizens taken Captive on the high Seas to bear Arms against their Country, to become the Executioners of their Friends and Brethren, or to fall themselves by their Hands.

He has excited domestic Insurrections amongst us, and has endeavoured to bring on the Inhabitants of our Frontiers, the merciless Indian Savages, whose known Rule of Warfare, is an undistinguished Destruction, of all Ages, Sexes and Conditions.

In every stage of these Oppressions we have Petitioned for Redress in the most humble Terms: Our repeated Petitions have been answered only by repeated Injury. A Prince, whose Character is thus marked by every act which may define a Tyrant, is unfit to be the Ruler of a free People.

Nor have we been wanting in Attentions to our British Brethren. We have warned them from Time to Time of Attempts by their Legislature to extend an unwarrantable Jurisdiction over us. We have reminded them of the Circumstances of our Emigration and Settlement here. We have appealed to their native Justice and Magnanimity, and we have conjured them by the Ties of our common Kindred to disavow these Usurpations, which, would inevitably interrupt our Connections and Correspondence. They too have been deaf to the Voice of Justice and of Consanguinity. We must, therefore, acquiesce in the Necessity, which denounces our Separation, and hold them, as we hold the rest of Mankind, Enemies in War, in Peace, Friends.

We, therefore, the Representatives of the UNITED STATES OF AMERICA, in GENERAL CONGRESS, Assembled, appealing to the Supreme Judge of the World for the Rectitude of our Intentions, do, in the Name, and by Authority of the good People of these Colonies, solemnly Publish and Declare, That these United Colonies are, and of Right ought to be, FREE AND INDEPENDENT STATES; that they are absolved from all Allegiance to the British Crown, and that all political Connection between them and the State of Great-Britain, is and ought to be totally dissolved; and that as FREE AND INDEPENDENT STATES, they have full Power to levy War, conclude Peace, contract Alliances, establish Commerce, and to do all other Acts and Things which INDEPENDENT STATES may of right do. And for the support of this Declaration, with a firm Reliance on the Protection of divine Providence, we mutually pledge to each other our Lives, our Fortunes, and our sacred Honor.

Signed by ORDER and in BEHALF of the CONGRESS,

JOHN HANCOCK, PRESIDENT.

ATTEST.
CHARLES THOMSON, SECRETARY.

PHILADELPHIA: PRINTED BY JOHN DUNLAP.

In CONGRESS, July 4, 1776.

A DECLARATION

By the REPRESENTATIVES of the

UNITED STATES OF AMERICA,

In GENERAL CONGRESS ASSEMBLED.

WHEN in the Courfe of human Events, it becomes neceſſary for one People to diſſolve the Political Bands which have connected them with another, and to aſſume among the Powers of the Earth, the ſeparate and equal Station to which the Laws of Nature and of Nature's God entitle them, a decent Reſpect to the Opinions of Mankind requires that they ſhould declare the cauſes which impel them to the Separation.

We hold theſe Truths to be ſelf-evident, that all Men are created equal, that they are endowed by their Creator with certain unalienable Rights, that among theſe are Life, Liberty, and the Purſuit of Happineſs—That to ſecure theſe Rights, Governments are inſtituted among Men, deriving their juſt Powers from the Conſent of the Governed, that whenever any Form of Government becomes deſtructive of theſe Ends, it is the Right of the People to alter or to aboliſh it, and to inſtitute new Government, laying its Foundation on ſuch Principles, and organizing

A copy of the U.S. Declaration of Independence. The declaration spells out unalienable rights that democratic governments are designed to protect, among them life and liberty. NARA

COMMAND ECONOMY

A command economy is an economic system in which the means of production are publicly owned and economic activity is controlled by a central authority that assigns quantitative production goals and allots raw materials to productive enterprises. In such a system, determining the proportion of total product used for investment rather than consumption becomes a centrally made political decision. After this decision has been made, the central planners work out the assortment of goods to be produced and the quotas for each enterprise. Consumers may influence the planners' decisions indirectly if the planners take into consideration the surpluses and shortages that have developed in the market. The only direct choice made by consumers, however, is among the commodities already produced.

Prices are also set by the central planners, but they do not serve, as in a market economy, as signals to producers of goods to increase or decrease production. Instead, they are used mainly as instruments of the central planners in their efforts to reconcile the total demand for consumer goods with the supply available, allowing also for revenues to the state.

The central authority in a command economy assigns production goals in terms of physical units and allocates physical quantities of raw materials to enterprises. The process for a large economy with millions of products is extremely complex and has encountered a number of difficulties in practice.

Central planning of this kind is not without apparent advantages, however, since it enables a government to mobilize resources quickly on a national scale during wartime or some other national emergency. But the costs of centralized policies are real and quite high. Moreover, it is often the case that much of the burden of these costs is shifted away from the government. One example is the military draft, which largely shifts the cost of mobilizing troops from the government to the draftees, who could be employed at a higher rate of pay elsewhere.

SELF-PRESERVATION

The first right of individuals and countries is self-preservation. The task of maintaining the country, however, is more complex than the individual's duty of self-preservation, for the country must seek to command the attachment of a community of citizens as well as to preserve itself from external violence. As the English political philosopher Thomas Hobbes insisted, civil war constitutes the greatest threat to governments, for it represents the dissolution of the "sovereign power." In modern terms, civil war signifies that the government has lost one of the basic attributes of political authority, namely its monopoly of force and its control over the use of violence. In a fundamental sense, political authority may be preserved from the threat of civil war only when there exists in the political community an agreement on the basic principles of the regime. Such a consensus is the result, among other things, of a shared ideology that gives fellow citizens a sense of communal belonging and recognizes interlocking values, interests, and beliefs. Ideology, in this sense, may be the product of many different forces. Sometimes it is associated with ancient customs, sometimes with religion, sometimes with severe dislocations or the sort of common need that has led to the formation of many nation-states, and sometimes with the fear of a common enemy. The ideological commitment that people call "patriotism" is typically the product of several of these forces.

Governments neglect at their peril the task of strengthening the ideological attachment of their citizens to the regime. In this sense, civic education should be counted among the essential functions of the state, for it is primarily through systems of education that citizens learn their duties. Indeed, as a number of sociological studies have shown, the process of political socialization that transforms people into citizens begins in kindergarten and grade school. Even more than this, education is the instrument by which governments further the cohesion of their societies and build the fundamental kinds of consensus that support their authority. It is not surprising, therefore, that national systems of education are often linked to central elements of the regimes. In France public education was traditionally mixed with the teachings of the Roman Catholic Church, and in Great Britain a private system of education supported the class divisions of society. In the United States a primarily secular form of public education traditionally used constitutional documents as the starting point of children's training in patriotism.

The preservation of the authority of the state also requires a governmental organization capable of imposing its jurisdiction on every part of the national territory. This

Elementary school students participating in a mock vote. Some experts believe that political socialization, or training in citizenship, should begin at an early age. Bill Bachmann/Photo Researchers/ Getty Images

involves the maintenance of means of communication, the use of administrative systems, and the employment of police forces capable of controlling domestic violence. The police function, like education, is often a key to the character of a regime. In Nazi Germany, Hitler's Brownshirts took over the operation of local and regional police systems and often supervised the administration of law in the streets. In the Soviet Union the security police acted to check any deviation from the policy of the party or state. In the United States the police powers are largely left in the hands of the 50 states and the local agencies of government. In addition, there are state militias that act, under the control of the governors of the various states, in moments of local emergency, such as riots or natural catastrophes. The Federal Bureau of Investigation (FBI), in some respects the equivalent of a national police force, is an agency established to carry out specific assignments dealing with a limited but important class of crimes. Since there is no comprehensive federal criminal code, there is not, strictly speaking, a federal police.

Governments must preserve themselves against external as well as domestic threats. For this purpose they maintain armed forces and carry on intelligence activities. They also try to prevent the entry of aliens who may be spies or terrorists, imprison or expel the agents of foreign powers, and embargo the export of materials that may aid a potential enemy. The ultimate means of preserving the state against external threats, of course, is war. In war, governments usually enlarge the scope of their domestic authority, by raising conscript forces, imprisoning conscientious objectors, subjecting aliens to internment, sentencing traitors to death, imposing extraordinary controls on the economy, censoring the press, compelling settlement of labour disputes, imposing internal-travel limitations, withholding passports, and providing for summary forms of arrest.

Many forces generate clashes between countries, including economic rivalry and disputes over trade, the desire to dominate strategic land or sea areas, religious or ideological conflict, and imperialistic ambition. All national governments develop organizations and policies to meet these and other situations. They have foreign ministries for the conduct of diplomatic relations with other countries, for representing the country in international organizations, and for negotiating treaties. Some governments conduct programs such as foreign aid, cultural exchange, and other activities designed to win goodwill abroad.

In the 20th century, relationships between governments were affected by a developing awareness that world peace and prosperity depend on multinational and international cooperation. The League of Nations and its successor, the United Nations, together with their associated agencies, represent major efforts to establish substitutes for traditional forms of diplomacy. Regional alliances and joint efforts, such as the Organization of American States, the North Atlantic Treaty Organization, the European Union, and the African Union, represent another type of cooperation between countries.

SUPERVISION AND RESOLUTION
OF CONFLICTS

The conflict of private interest is the leading characteristic of the political process in constitutional democracies, and the supervision, mediation, arbitration, and adjudication of such conflicts are among the key functions of their governments. Representative institutions are themselves a device for the resolution of conflict. Thus, elections in constitutional democracies provide opportunities for mass participation in a process of open debate and public decision; assemblies, congresses, and other parliamentary institutions provide for public hearings on major issues of policy and require formal deliberative procedures at different stages of the legislative process; and political parties integrate a variety of interests and effect compromises on policy that win acceptance from many different groups.

If the interests that compete in the political process are too narrow or restricted, efforts may be made to control or change the rules of competition. Thus, laws have been enacted that seek to prevent discrimination from locking women and minority groups out of the democratic process. The franchise has been extended to all groups—including women, minorities, and 18-year-olds—and government bodies such as courts and administrative agencies enforce legislation against groups considered to be too large or monopolistic.

An energy activist addressing attendees of a U.S. State Department public hearing on proposed oil pipeline construction. Democracies generally provide public forums wherein citizens can state their opinions. Bloomberg via Getty Images

Judicial processes offer a means by which some disputes in society are settled according to rule and legal authority, rather than by political struggle. In all advanced societies, law is elaborated in complex codes governing rights and duties and procedural methods, and court systems are employed that adjudicate disputes in terms of the law. In constitutional systems such as the United States, the judiciary is deeply involved in the process of public decision making. Indeed, the courts actually produce much of the substantive law that bears on private individuals and economic groups in society.

REGULATION OF THE ECONOMY

Government regulation of economic life is not a new development. The national mercantilist systems of the 18th century provided for regulation of the production, distribution, and export of goods by government ministries. Even during the 19th century, governments continued to intervene in the economy. The government of the United States, for example, from its inception in 1789, allotted funds or subsidies for the support of agriculture, maintained a system of tariffs for its own revenue and the support of domestic manufacturers, patronized the arts and sciences, and engaged in various kinds of public works to advance commerce and promote the general welfare. In France even more elaborate governmental schemes of economic regulation were practiced throughout the 19th century, including a variety of socialist experiments such as the Public Workshops that the French utopian socialist Louis Blanc established in Paris in 1848. In Britain the various factory acts of the 19th century represented an effort by government to improve slightly the working conditions in industry.

After World War II the ability of a government to regulate or control the economy became one of the chief tests of its success, and regulatory agencies multiplied to the point at which they were often referred to as "the fourth branch of government." The extent of the controls imposed on the economy is one of the principal distinctions between capitalist, socialist, and communist systems. In communist countries it is a matter of doctrine that the means of production should be owned and therefore controlled by the state. In Britain the Labour governments nationalized some major industries, including coal, steel, and the railroads, prompted partly by socialist doctrine and partly by the failure of British industry to remain competitive in international markets. This process was then partly reversed when the Conservative Party became ascendent in the late 1970s. In the United States the government has involved itself in the economy primarily through its regulatory powers. In France the government has gone farther and has engaged in national economic planning in cooperation with private business organizations.

The regulation of industrial conditions and of labour-management relations has been a major concern of most Western governments. In the United States the first regulatory efforts in this field were made during the Progressive era at the turn of the 20th century, when the wages, hours, and working conditions of women and children in industry became a matter of public scandal. A little later the conditions, hours, food, and wages of merchant seamen were brought under government regulation; an eight-hour day was set for railway crews; and workmen's compensation laws were instituted. With the Great Depression in the 1930s, minimum wages were introduced for workers in many industries, hours of work were set, and the right to collective bargaining was given legal sanction.

Regulation of transportation has been another major activity in most Western political systems, beginning with the railroads. In the United States their monopolistic

Men selling and reading Myanmar's state-run newspaper, New Light of Myanmar, March 2010. Authoritarian governments frequently control the media, thus manipulating what information reaches the public. AFP/Getty Images

practices attracted the criticism of agricultural interests and led eventually to the Interstate Commerce Act of 1887, which regulated railroad rates. Subsequent legislation covered the hours, conditions, and wages of railroad employees, among other things. Other modes of land and air transportation have since been brought under regulatory controls implemented by government agencies.

In many European countries, major facilities of communication—including telephone, radio, and television—are partly or wholly owned and operated by the government. In the United States, most of these facilities have remained in private hands, although they are regulated by the Federal Communications Commission. The regulation by government of important instruments of public opinion such as newspapers, radio, television, and the Internet has important implications for the freedoms of speech and press and other individual rights. In the United States and Great Britain, government censorship of the press and other media has been restricted to matters of national security. This is also generally true of other Western constitutional democracies. In many of the less-developed countries with authoritarian governments, very extensive controls are imposed on the press, and government-owned newspapers are often the principal sources of political news.

Other forms of government regulation of the economy involve the use of taxes and tariffs, the regulation of weights and measures, and the issuance of money.

PROTECTION OF POLITICAL AND SOCIAL RIGHTS

To some extent, all modern governments assume responsibility for protecting the political and social rights of their citizens. The protection of individual rights has taken two principal forms: (1) the protection of liberty in the face of governmental oppression and (2) the protection of individual rights against hostile majorities and minorities. From the 1960s to the mid-1980s the sphere of public discussion in the Soviet Union was gradually, though erratically, widened. While this widening never extended to the purely political, some of the sociological discussion allowed served to set the intellectual stage

General Secretary of the Soviet Communist Party Mikhail Gorbachev meets with car factory workers in Moscow in 1985. Economic and political reforms were the hallmarks of Gorbachev's perestroika initiative. Keystone-France/Gamma Keystone via Getty Images

for the Gorbachev period of radical reform (perestroika). Although the Soviet Union suppressed most expression of political opinion until the late 1980s, domination by a central authority protected the basic human rights of some groups from violent rival minorities. On a larger scale, this is also what suppressed many long-standing rivalries in eastern Europe during the Cold War. The degree of repression in the former communist states varied from country to country and changed with time after the death of Stalin.

In the second half of the 20th century in the United States, the rights of the criminally accused were expanded in such cases as *Gideon* v. *Wainwright* (1963), in which the Supreme Court ruled that indigent defendants had a right to a court-appointed attorney, and *Miranda* v. *Arizona* (1966), in which the court specified a code of conduct for police interrogations of criminal suspects held in custody. After the Supreme Court's ruling in *Brown* v. *Board of Education of Topeka* in 1954, the national government acted to bar legal discrimination against ethnic minorities, as well as women, people with disabilities, gays and lesbians, and the elderly. Indeed, in the second half of the 20th century, many (but not all) freedoms detailed in the Bill of Rights (the first 10 amendments to the Constitution) were extended. By the early 21st century, however, as the Supreme Court assumed a more conservative orientation, it shifted its focus away from the expansion of minority rights. For example, on issues of race, the Supreme Court ruled in the Bollinger decisions (2003) and in *Ricci* v. *DeStefano* (2009) that, while affirmative action policies aiming to provide minority groups with broader employment or educational opportunities could still be used, such policies were not valid if race was the determining factor.

RICCI V. DESTEFANO

Ricci v. *DeStefano* was a legal case alleging racial discrimination that was decided by the U.S. Supreme Court on June 29, 2009. The court's decision, which agreed that the plaintiffs were unfairly kept from job promotions because of their race, was expected to have widespread ramifications for affirmative action and civil rights law.

The case arose after the New Haven, Conn., fire department offered a promotional examination to its firefighters in 2003. Seventy-seven firefighters took the exam, but none of the 19 African Americans among them earned results deemed high enough to warrant a promotion. Fearing a lawsuit alleging racial discrimination, department officials discarded the results and determined that they would not promote anyone based solely on the results of the written test. A racial discrimination lawsuit was then brought against the city of New Haven by firefighters—including 18 whites and one Latino—whose test results would have qualified them for promotion.

The man at the centre of the lawsuit was Frank Ricci, a white firefighter who testified that he had studied for several hours a day and had paid a friend to record textbooks onto tape for him so that he could overcome his dyslexia in order to do well on the test. New Haven's mayor, John DeStefano, was named as one of the respondents in the lawsuit. Attorneys for the city of New Haven argued that it was unfair to perceive the department's action as racial discrimination because they were trying to comply with Title VII of the Civil Rights Act (1964), which bans discriminatory practices by employers.

In its 5–4 decision, the Supreme Court reversed the decision of the Second Circuit court, arguing that the Latino and white firefighters had been unfairly denied promotions because of their race. Justice Anthony Kennedy, who delivered the opinion of the majority, wrote: "Fear of litigation alone cannot justify the City's reliance on race to the detriment of individuals who passed the examinations and qualified for promotions. Discarding the test results was impermissible under Title VII." The dissenting position, written by Justice Ruth Bader Ginsburg, held that the white firefighters "had no vested right to promotion. Nor have other persons received promotions in preference to them."

Another type of government regulation bearing on the individual concerns the law of immigration and emigration. The great mass migrations of the 19th and early 20th centuries came to an abrupt halt after 1914 with the proliferation of government controls on the freedom of movement across national boundaries. After some later liberalization, immigration to the industrialized states again saw increased restrictions near the end of the 20th century.

PROVISION OF GOODS AND SERVICES

All modern governments participate directly in the economy, purchasing goods, operating industries, providing services, and promoting various economic activities. One of the indispensable functions of government—national defense—has made governments the most important consumers of goods, and they have not hesitated to use their resulting pricing, purchasing, and contracting powers to achieve various economic aims. In efforts to avoid dependence on private sources of strategic goods and defense materials, some governments have taken a further step and established their own military production plants. In wartime, governments have assumed control over entire industries and have subjected the work force to military direction in addition to rationing goods and regulating prices.

In nearly all political systems, certain functions are recognized as primarily public, or belonging to the government, although some aspects of these services may be handled by the private sector. In addition to national defense, public functions include the maintenance of domestic peace, public education, fire protection, traffic control, conservation of natural resources, flood control, and postal services. Many governments have assumed responsibility for additional commercial operations, even in nonsocialist countries. The sale of electric power, for example, is one of the established enterprising functions of national, state, and local governments in the United States and Canada. Municipally owned power utilities exist in many cities in North America. A number of states in the U.S. have public power districts, and the U.S. government markets power through the Tennessee Valley Authority, the Bureau of Reclamation, and several other agencies. Another range of functions, such as lending and insurance, are performed by other national agencies, including the Veterans Administration, the Federal Deposit Insurance Corporation, and the Federal Housing Administration.

Other miscellaneous enterprises in which governments are involved include the provision of health care, the operation of public transport facilities, the development of public works, airport and port maintenance, and water-supply systems. In Great Britain the government operates hospitals and provides medical care under the

A New York postal worker delivering mail to multiple mailboxes. The United States Postal Service is an agency of the U.S. federal government. Bloomberg via Getty Images

National Health Service. In the United States many state and local governments operate hospitals on a commercial basis while providing some charity care. At the local level in the United States, the Port Authority of New York and New Jersey constructs and operates bridges, terminals, and airports. The states in the Delaware Basin joined in a compact to establish an agency to control the use of water from the basin, institute programs to prevent pollution, provide recreation facilities, transmit and sell hydroelectric power, and provide watershed management. Cities in the United States and Canada operate dozens of urban transit systems, hundreds of municipal gas utilities, and thousands of water-supply systems. Cities are also generally responsible for garbage disposal, and many cities manage parks and recreational amenities, such as golf courses. Finally, a number of state governments control the distribution of alcohol.

PUBLIC ADMINISTRATION

While the functional objectives of government administration vary from system to system, all countries that are technologically developed have evolved systems of public administration. A number of common features may be detected in all such systems. The first is the hierarchical, or pyramidal, character of the organization by which a single chief executive oversees a few subordinates, who in turn oversee their chief subordinates, who are in turn responsible for overseeing other subordinates, and so on until a great structure of personnel is integrated and focused on the components of a particular program. A second common feature is the division of labour or specialization within the organization. Each individual in the hierarchy has specialized responsibilities and tasks. A third feature is the maintenance of detailed official records and the existence of precise paper procedures through which the personnel of the system communicate with each other and with the public. Finally, tenure of office is also characteristic of all public bureaucracies.

The various national civil services, despite their similarities, also show important differences, particularly in the way in which individuals are recruited and in the status accorded them in the political system. The British civil service, for example, has traditionally been composed of three classes, or grades—clerical, executive, and administrative. Administrative civil servants, the highest grade, are recruited by examination from among recent university graduates. The top managers of the different government ministries are drawn from this elite group. They remain in office despite changes in government and are accorded immense prestige. The U.S. civil service is organized into more than a dozen grades. Although promotion from the lower grades is the typical means by which positions in the top grades are filled, there is also a flow of individuals into senior positions from private business and the professions. The U.S. equivalent of the administrative civil servant in Britain is usually a political appointee recruited by each new administration from private life or from a position in politics.

CHAPTER 5

Development and Change in Political Systems

Students of political systems grapple with a subject matter that is today in constant flux. They must deal not only with the major processes of growth, decay, and breakdown but also with a ceaseless ferment of adaptation and adjustment. The magnitude and variety of the changes that have occurred in the world's political systems since the early 20th century suggest the dimensions of the problem. Great empires have disintegrated, and nation-states have emerged, flourished briefly, and then vanished. World wars have twice transformed the international system, and new ideologies have swept the world and shook established groups from power. All but a few countries experienced at least one revolution and many countries two or more. Domestic politics in every system were contorted by social strife and economic crisis, and everywhere the nature of political life was changed by novel forms of political activity, new means of mass communication, the enlargement of popular participation in politics, the rise of new political issues, the extension of the scope of governmental activity, the threat of nuclear war and international terrorism, and innumerable other social, economic, and technical developments.

CAUSES OF STABILITY AND INSTABILITY

Although it is possible to identify a number of factors that obviously have a great deal to do with contemporary development and change in the world's political systems—industrialization, population growth, the "revolution of rising expectations" in the less developed countries, and international tensions—there is no generally accepted theory to explain the causes of political change. Some social scientists have followed Aristotle's view that political instability is generally the result of a situation in which the distribution of wealth fails to correspond with the distribution of political power and have echoed his conclusion that the most stable type of political system is one based on a large middle class. Others have adopted Marxist theories of economic determinism that view all political change as the result of changes in the mode of production. Still others have focused on governing elites and their composition and have seen in the alienation of the elite from the mass the prime cause of revolutions and other forms of violent political change.

In the discussion that follows, a distinction is drawn between unstable and stable political systems, and an attempt is made to suggest ways of understanding the processes of political development and change.

UNSTABLE POLITICAL SYSTEMS

In modern times, the great majority of the world's political systems have experienced one form or another of internal warfare leading to violent collapse of the governments in power. Certain crisis situations seem to increase the likelihood of this kind of breakdown. Wars and, more particularly, national military defeats have been decisive in prompting many revolutions. The Paris Commune of 1871, the Russian revolutions of 1905 and 1917, Hitler's overthrow of the Weimar Constitution in Germany, and the revolutions in China all occurred in the aftermath of national military disasters. Many factors in such a situation—including the cheapening of human life, the

THE COMMUNE OF PARIS

The Commune of Paris, also called the Paris Commune, was an insurrection by the city of Paris against the French government from March 18 to May 28, 1871. It occurred in the wake of France's defeat in the Franco-German War and the collapse of Napoleon III's Second Empire (1852–70).

The National Assembly, which was elected in February 1871 to conclude a peace with Germany, had a royalist majority, reflecting the conservative attitude of the provinces. The republican Parisians feared that the National Assembly meeting in Versailles would restore the monarchy.

To ensure order in Paris, Adolphe Thiers, executive head of the provisional national government, decided to disarm the National Guard (composed largely of workers who fought during the siege of Paris by the Germans in September 1870). On March 18, resistance broke out in Paris in response to an attempt to remove the cannons of the guard overlooking the city. Then, on March 26, municipal elections, organized by the central committee of the guard, resulted in victory for the revolutionaries, who formed the Commune government. The program that the Commune adopted, despite its internal divisions, called for measures reminiscent of 1793 (e.g., end of support for religion and use of the Revolutionary calendar) and a limited number of social measures (e.g., a 10-hour workday).

With the quick suppression of communes that arose at Lyon, Saint-Étienne, Marseille, and Toulouse, the Commune of Paris alone faced the opposition of the Versailles government. But the Fédérés, as the insurgents were called, were unable to organize themselves militarily and take the offensive, and, on May 21, government troops entered an undefended section of Paris. During *la semaine sanglante*, or "bloody week," that followed, the regular troops crushed the opposition of the Communards, who in their defense set up barricades in the streets and burned public buildings. About 20,000 insurrectionists were killed, along with about 750 government troops. In the aftermath of the Commune, the government took harsh repressive action: about 38,000 were arrested and more than 7,000 were deported.

dislocation of population, the ready availability of arms, the disintegration of authority, the discrediting of the national leadership, material scarcities, and a sense of wounded national pride—contribute to the creation of an atmosphere in which radical political change and violent mass action are acceptable to large numbers of people.

Economic crises are another common stimulus to revolutionary outbreaks, for they produce not only the obvious pressures of material scarcity and deprivation but also a threat to the individual's social position, a sense of insecurity and uncertainty as to the future, and an aggravation of the relationships among social classes. A severe national economic crisis works, in much the same way as a military disaster, to discredit the existing leadership and regime.

Another triggering factor is the outbreak of revolutions in other political systems. Revolutions have a tendency to spread. The Spanish Revolution of 1820, for example, had repercussions in Naples, Portugal, and Piedmont. The French Revolution of July 1830 provoked similar outbreaks in Poland and Belgium, and the Russian Revolution of 1917 was followed by a dozen other revolutions. The colonial liberation movements in Africa, Southeast Asia, and elsewhere after World War II appear to have involved a similar chain reaction, as did the popular revolutions in some countries of the Middle East in the early 21st century during the so-called Arab Spring.

Crisis situations test the stability of political systems in extremely revealing ways, for they place extraordinary demands on the political leadership and the structure and processes of the system. Since the quality of the political leadership is often decisive, those systems that provide methods of selecting able leaders and replacing them possess important advantages. Although leadership ability is not guaranteed by any method of selection, it is more

Tunisian citizens demonstrating in front of the government palace in Tunis, January 2011. Demonstrations in Tunisia started the Arab Spring pro-democracy movement that swept across the Middle East. Fethi Belaid/AFP/Getty Images

likely to be found where there is free competition for leadership positions. The availability of established methods of replacing leaders is equally, if not more, important, for the result of crises is often to disgrace the leaders in power, and, if they cannot be replaced easily, their continued incumbency may discredit the whole regime. Also important are the stamina and resolve of the ruling elite. It is often said that a united elite, firmly believing in the justice of its own cause and determined to employ every measure to maintain its power, will not be overthrown. Most revolutions have gotten under way not when the oppression was greatest but only after the government had lost confidence in its own cause.

Other conditions of the survival of political systems relate to the effectiveness of the structures and processes of government in meeting the demands placed on them. Political systems suffer violent breakdown when channels of communication fail to function effectively, when institutional structures and processes fail to resolve conflicts among demands and to implement acceptable policies, and when the system ceases to be viewed as responsive by individuals and groups making demands on it. Usually, a system fails over a period of some time to satisfy persistent and widespread demands. Then, exposed to the additional strains of a crisis situation, it is unable to maintain itself. Revolutions and other forms of violent collapse are thus rarely sudden catastrophes but rather the result of a process of considerable duration that comes to its climax when the system is most vulnerable.

Unstable political systems are those that prove vulnerable to crisis pressures and that break down into various forms of internal warfare. The fundamental causes of such failures appear to be the lack of a widespread sense of the legitimacy of state authority and the absence of some general agreement on appropriate forms of political action. Governments suffer their gravest handicap when they must govern without consent or when the legitimacy of the regime is widely questioned. This is often the case in systems that have experienced prolonged civil war, that are torn by tensions among different national or ethnic groups, or in which there are divisions along sharply drawn ideological or class lines. The problem is often most acute where there is a pretender to the throne, a government in exile, a neighbouring state sympathetic to a rebel cause, or some other focus for the loyalty of dissidents.

To some degree, also, the problem of legitimacy confronts all newly established regimes. Many of the post-colonial countries of Africa and Asia, for example, found it a source of great difficulty. Often they emulated the form of Western institutions but failed to achieve their spirit. Borrowing eclectically from Western political philosophies and systems of law, they created constitutional frameworks and institutional structures that lacked meaning to their citizens and that failed to generate loyalty or a sense that government exercises rightful powers.

Closely related to the problem of legitimacy as a cause of the breakdown of political systems is the absence of a fundamental consensus on what is appropriate political behaviour. A regime is fortunate if there are well-established, open channels of political action and settled procedures for resolving grievances. Although the importance of such "rules of the game" is that they allow change to occur in mainly peaceful ways, stable political systems often show surprising tolerance for potentially violent forms of political behaviour, such as strikes, boycotts, and mass demonstrations. Such forms of political behaviour

Hissène Habré (in white), self-appointed ruler of Chad, with fellow African dictator Mobutu Sese Seko (animal-print hat) in 1983. Habré's corrupt government was toppled by one of his military advisors in 1990. Pierre Perrin/Gamma-Rapho/Getty Images

are not permitted in systems where there are no agreed limits to the role of violence and where there is a high risk that violence may escalate to the point of actual warfare. If the government cannot count upon widespread support for peaceful political procedures, it must restrict many kinds of political action. Such restriction, of course, inhibits still more the development of open methods of citizen participation in politics and adds to tension between the government and the people.

STABLE POLITICAL SYSTEMS

The simplest definition of a stable political system is one that survives through crises without internal warfare. Several types of political systems have done so, including despotic monarchies, militarist regimes, and other authoritarian and totalitarian systems. After 1868, in the period of the restoration regime under the Meiji emperor, Japan succeeded, without major political breakdowns, in building an industrial state and developing commercial structures that transformed traditional Japanese society. This achievement was based on the development of centralized patterns of political control and the growth of a type of authoritarianism involving the rule of a military elite. Similarly, since the early 20th century some totalitarian regimes have demonstrated an impressive capability for survival. The key to their success has been their ability to control social development, to manage and prevent change, and to bring under governmental direction all the forces that may result in innovations that are threatening to the system.

In some systems, survival does not depend on the detailed management of the society or close governmental control over social processes but is the result of sensitive political response to the forces of change, of flexible

Japanese women working in a silk plant during the Meiji period (1868–1912). Industry in Japan grew at this time under a stable monarchy, which was led by an emperor. Buyenlarge/Archive Photos/Getty Images

adjustment of the structures of the system to meet the pressures of innovation, and of open political processes that allow gradual and orderly development. Much of the Western democratic world has achieved peaceful progress in this way, despite new political philosophies, population increases, industrial and technological innovations, and many other social and economic stresses.

Such evolutionary change is possible when representative institutions provide effective channels for the communication of demands and criticisms to governments that rely upon majority support. The election of legislators and executive officials, competition between political parties, constitutional guarantees of freedom of speech and press, the right of petition, and many other structures and procedures perform this function in contemporary constitutional democracies. In such systems, social and economic problems are quickly transformed into issues in the open arenas of politics, and governments are obliged to shape policies that reflect a variety of pressures and effect compromises among many conflicting demands.

The representative mechanisms that have produced evolutionary change in Western constitutional democracies are themselves subject to a continuous process of adjustment and mutation. Indeed, representative institutions must develop in ways that reflect social and economic developments in the society or they will lose their legitimacy in the minds of the people. In political systems such as the United States, for example, subtle shifts in the function and relative power of different institutions are continuously being made and, over time, produce entirely new structures and very different patterns of institutional behaviour. It is as a result of this process that the presidency has accumulated a range of new powers that have given it primacy among the branches of American government. This process also explains the growth of administrative agencies that perform both legislative and judicial functions. This process of dynamic adjustment is crucial, for institutions that remain static in a changing society are unable to serve as agencies of evolutionary change.

TYPES OF POLITICAL CHANGE

The study of political change is difficult, for change occurs in many different ways and at many different points in the political system. One may distinguish several major types of change.

RADICAL REVOLUTION

First are changes of the most fundamental type—transformations not only of the structure of government but of the whole polity. Such change is not limited to political life but transforms also the social order, the moral basis, and the values of the whole society. Drastic change of this kind occurred in the four great revolutions of the modern era—the Glorious Revolution of the 17th century, the American Revolution, the French Revolution, and the Russian Revolution. These movements had the most profound effect on social and political life, permanently altering the beliefs by which people live. Their consequences were felt not only in the societies in which they occurred but also in many other political systems, in which, as a result of their example, revolutions of an equally fundamental character occurred.

Each of these major revolutions was something of a world revolution, for it resulted in a basic change in the ways in which people in all political systems viewed the nature of politics and the purpose of political life. The independence movements in the colonial empires after World War II, for example, were fuelled by those principles

THE GLORIOUS REVOLUTION

The Glorious Revolution (also called the Revolution of 1688, or the Bloodless Revolution) resulted in the deposition of King James II of England and the accession of his daughter Mary II and her husband, William III, prince of Orange and stadholder of the Netherlands.

After the accession of James II in 1685, his overt Roman Catholicism alienated the majority of the population. The birth of a son to James's Roman Catholic queen, Mary of Modena (June), promised an indefinite continuance of his religious policy and brought discontent to a head. Seven eminent Englishmen, including one bishop and six prominent politicians of both Whig and Tory persuasions invited William of Orange to come to England with an army to redress the nation's grievances.

William was both James's nephew and his son-in-law, and, until the birth of James's son, his wife, Mary, was heir apparent. William's chief concern was to check the overgrowth of

Depiction of King James II receiving the news that William of Orange had arrived in England to dethrone him. The Bridgeman Art Library/ Getty Images

French power in Europe, and he welcomed England's aid. Thus, he accepted their invitation. Landing at Brixham on Tor Bay (November 5), he advanced slowly on London, as support fell away from James II. James's daughter Anne and his best general, John Churchill, were among the deserters to William's camp. Thereupon James fled to France.

William was now asked to carry on the government and summon a Parliament. When this Convention Parliament met (Jan. 22, 1689), it agreed to treat James's flight as an abdication and to offer the Crown, with an accompanying Declaration of Right, to William and Mary jointly. Both gift and conditions were accepted. Thereupon the convention turned itself into a proper Parliament and large parts of the Declaration into a Bill of Rights. This bill gave the succession to Mary's sister, Anne, in default of issue to Mary, barred Roman Catholics from the throne, abolished the Crown's power to suspend laws, and declared a standing army illegal in time of peace.

The settlement marked a considerable triumph for Whig views. If no Roman Catholic could be king, then no kingship could be unconditional. The adoption of the exclusionist solution lent support to John Locke's contention that government was in the nature of a social contract between the king and his people represented in parliament. The revolution permanently established Parliament as the ruling power of England.

of individual liberty and representative government that were once the slogans of 18th-century American and French revolutionaries. Marxist revolutionary concepts emphasizing economic progress and radical social change shaped the development of many new countries. The continuing impact of such ideas is an example of another way in which fundamental political change occurs. The nature of a political system may be transformed not suddenly or violently in the course of revolution but by the gradual, corrosive influence of ideas and by the accumulating impact of different political philosophies.

STRUCTURAL REVISION

A second type of change involves alterations to the structure of the political system. Such change is not fundamental, in the sense of a basic transformation of the nature of the regime, but it may produce great shifts in policy and other political outcomes. Because the structure of a political system—that is, its formal and informal institutional arrangements—is a major determinant of policy outcomes, it is frequently the target of political action of various kinds. The political activist, the reformer, and the revolutionary share the recognition that the policies of a government may be effectively changed by adjusting the institutional forms through which the government acts.

In some systems, structural change has been accomplished by legal means. In the United States, for example, such major institutional reforms as the direct election of the Senate and the limitation on presidential terms were made by constitutional amendment, and in Britain the various reforms of Parliament were accomplished by statute. In other systems, structural changes are often achieved by revolution and other violence.

CHANGE OF LEADERS

A third type of political change involves the replacement of leaders. Again, the recognition that changing the personnel of a government may be an effective way of changing government policy prompts many kinds of political action, ranging from election contests to political assassination and various forms of coup d'etat.

An activist attending a hearing on the U.S. military's "Don't Ask, Don't Tell" policy. The policy was repealed in 2011, allowing gay men and women in the armed forces to serve openly. Mandel Ngan/AFP/Getty Images

In some systems the existence of established means of changing political leaderships works to prevent violent types of political action. In the United States, for example, the quadrennial contests for the presidency afford a constitutional opportunity to throw the whole executive leadership out of office. At the other extreme, the coup d'etat leads to the abrupt, often violent replacement of national executives. Although it is a type of revolution, the coup d'etat usually does not involve prolonged struggle or popular participation. Indeed, after seizing office, the principal aim of the leaders of the coup is usually the restoration of public order. The coup d'etat occasionally develops into much more than the replacement of one set of governmental leaders by another and may prove to be the initial stage of a truly revolutionary process — e.g., the coups d'etat that initiated communist rule in Czechoslovakia in 1948 and ended King Farouk I's regime in Egypt in 1952.

CHANGE OF POLICIES

Government policy itself may be an important agency of political change. The social and economic policies of Franklin D. Roosevelt's New Deal and the socialist programs implemented by the British Labour Party after 1945 are examples. In both cases, government policies resulted in far-reaching modifications to the functioning of the political system: a vast expansion in the role of government in the economy, the use of taxes to redistribute wealth, an increase in the political influence of organized labour, and the implementation of national programs of social welfare. Major policy change of this type, of course, is often a response to widespread pressures and demands that, if not satisfied by the system, may intensify and lead to various forms of violent political action. At other times,

Men from the Civilian Conservation Corps (CCC) clear brush and plant new trees in 1935. The CCC was part of Franklin D. Roosevelt's New Deal, a socioeconomic program that greatly expanded the role of the federal government in the U.S. economy. FPG/Archive Photos/Getty Images

however, policy changes are imposed by a government to achieve the political, social, and economic goals of a single class, of an elite, or of the political leadership itself.

Many important questions remain as to the reasons for change, the ways in which change occurs, and the effects of change. Political scientists are still not completely certain, for example, why some systems have managed to avoid violent political change for considerable periods, while in other systems change is typically accomplished through coups d'etat, revolutions, and other forms of internal warfare. As suggested above, the explanation may have much to do with the existence in countries such as the United States and Great Britain of well-established political institutions that permit peaceful change, the presence in the population of widely shared attitudes toward the government, and the existence of basic agreement on the legitimacy of state authority. Clearly, however, other factors are also involved. Perhaps one of the chief goals of the study of political systems should be to determine as exactly as possible the conditions and prerequisites of those forms of change that permit the peaceful and evolutionary development of human society.

Conclusion

The notion of a political system embraces not only the formal legal institutions and norms that constitute a state or other polity but also the ways in which such institutions and norms function or are applied in the real world. The traditional discipline of constitutional analysis is concerned with the former, more theoretical aspects of political systems, while the various (and more recent) fields of political science are occupied with the latter, more empirical or applied aspects.

Nation-states constitute the most ubiquitous and important type of political system in the modern world, but other types have been predominant historically, and (with a few exceptions) continue to exist today. Examples include empires; leagues; federations and confederations; supranational organizations; subnational states, provinces, and regions; cities; villages; and tribal governments. The political systems of modern nation-states may be divided between those in which political authority is shared between a national or central government and various subnational governments (a federal system) and those in which it is not (a unitary system). Nation-states, as well as other political systems, also may be classified according to mode of succession (e.g., hereditary, as in many monarchies and empires, or by election) or purported "stage of development," though the latter approach has sometimes invited charges of parochialism.

Some of the basic forms of government recognized today were identified by Aristotle in his classification of states (in his day, city-states) according to the number and aims of their rulers. Philosophers and political theorists of the Renaissance and early-modern period posited other forms, naturally reflecting the predominant political systems of their times, though none of their classifications was as influential as Aristotle's. The basic forms of national governments of the modern period are monarchy, dictatorship, oligarchy, and constitutional democracy.

Modern national political systems typically comprise multiple levels of government, principally including, in addition to the national level, a state or regional level and a local level. All levels of government carry out executive, legislative, and judicial functions, though there are not always distinct branches of government answering to those functions. Systems in which such branches exist are said to display a separation of powers among the branches. Some of the broader functions of any government are self-preservation (or preservation of the state), supervision and resolution of private conflicts, regulation of the economy, protection of individual rights, and provision of goods and services.

Change and development in political systems comprise the birth, death, or transformation of particular governments through revolution, structural or institutional change, modification of government policy, or the replacement of leaders. Unstable systems are susceptible to radical changes, which are usually precipitated by a military or economic crisis after a prolonged failure to carry out basic government functions or address popular demands and grievances. Stable systems are able to withstand such crises, either through ruthless oppression or the operation of institutions and processes that effectively manage internal conflicts and allow for evolutionary change in response to continual social, economic, technological, and intellectual challenges.

Political systems have been studied by Western philosophers, political theorists, historians, and political and social scientists since the time of Aristotle. Yet, despite a wealth of empirical data gleaned especially from studies of the last two centuries, there is still much about political systems that is poorly understood. For example, although numerous and varied correlates of political stability and instability have been identified, there is still no generally accepted theory of political change. Because of their great complexity, such fundamental questions concerning the nature of political systems are likely to challenge political scientists for some time to come.

autocracy A system of government in which one person holds unlimited power.

autonomous Having the right or power of self-government.

canton One of the states of the Swiss confederation.

coup d'etat The sudden, violent overthrow of an existing government by a small group.

decentralization The delegation of power from a central authority to regional or local authorities.

diffidatio A renunciation of faith or allegiance, as between a feudal lord and king.

empirical Relying on observation or experience.

feudalism The system of political organization based upon the relation of lord to vassal, with all land held in fee.

interest group A group of citizens gathered together to influence public policy.

megalopolis A densely populated region centred on a city or group of cities.

moiety One of two basic complementary tribal subdivisions.

monarchy A system of government having a hereditary chief of state for life, whose powers vary from nominal to absolute.

nation-state A form of political organization under which a group of relatively similar people, usually occupying a definite territory, live in an independent and self-governing fashion.

ochlocracy Government by the mob; mob rule.

oligarchy A system of government in which a select few exercise power for their own benefit.

polis A Greek city-state.

proletariat The class of industrial workers who lack their own means of production and hence sell their labour to live.

republic A system of government in which supreme power resides in a body of citizens entitled to vote, and is exercised by elected officers and representatives responsible to those citizens.

sociopolitical Involving a combination of social and political factors.

sovereignty The state of being independent and practicing self-rule.

succession The act or process by which an individual exercises the right, following another, to property, title, or leadership.

supranational Transcending national boundaries, authority, or interests.

totalitarianism The political concept that citizens should be totally subject to an absolute state authority.

welfare state A concept of government in which the state plays a key role in the protection and promotion of the economic and social well-being of its citizens.

Bibliography

Perhaps the single best introduction to the subjects covered in this book is *Mary Hawkesworth* and *Maurice Kogan* (eds.), *Encyclopedia of Government and Politics*, 2nd ed., 2 vol. (2004). Other excellent general works include *Anton Bebler* and *Jim Seroka* (eds.), *Contemporary Political Systems* (1990); and *Robert A. Dahl* and *Bruce Stinebrickner*, *Modern Political Analysis*, 6th ed. (2002). *Gabriel A. Almond* et al. (eds.), *Comparative Politics Today: A World View*, 9th ed., update (2010), is also of interest. Country-specific data can be found in *J. Denis Derbyshire* and *Ian Derbyshire*, *Political Systems of the World*, 3rd ed., 2 vol. (1999). A leading modern effort to develop types and models of political systems is *Gaetano Mosca, A Short History of Political Philosophy* (1972; originally published in Italian, 1931). A classic treatment of the empires of the ancient world may be found in *Arnold J. Toynbee, A Study of History*, 12 vol. (1934–61). *Gerard J. Mangone, A Short History of International Organization* (1954, reprinted 1975), is a convenient reference covering the development of many 20th-century supranational political institutions. The phenomenon of nationalism is treated in *E.J. Hobsbawm, Nations and Nationalism Since 1780*, 2nd ed. (1992). Useful comparative studies of local government are presented in *J.A. Chandler* (ed.), *Local Government in Liberal Democracies: An Introductory Survey* (1993). Worthy studies of modernization and political development include *Samuel P. Huntington, The Third Wave: Democratization in the Late Twentieth Century* (1991); and *Robert H. Jackson* and *Alan James* (eds.), *States*

139

in a Changing World: A Contemporary Analysis (1993). Two of the best introductions to the study of different forms of government are *Barrington Moore, Jr., Social Origins of Dictatorship and Democracy* (1966); and *Larry Diamond* and *Marc F. Plattner* (eds.), *Capitalism, Socialism, and Democracy Revisited* (1993). An excellent introduction to the problem of the relationship between different levels of government is offered in *Carl J. Friedrich, Man and His Government* (1963), especially part 5, "Ranges and Levels of Government." A short introduction to the divisions of government, suitable for the beginning student, is *Roy C. Macridis, Modern Political Regimes: Patterns and Institutions* (1986). Works dealing with the functions of various governments include *John H. Goldthorpe* (ed.), *Order and Conflict in Contemporary Capitalism* (1984); and *Peter Gourevitch, Politics in Hard Times: Comparative Responses to International Economic Crises* (1986). Development and change in various political systems are discussed in *Clifford Geertz* (ed.), *Old Societies and New States* (1963); and *Daniel Chirot, Social Change in the Modern Era* (1986).

Index

A

Achaean League, 5, 6–7
African Union, 102
American Revolution, 126, 128
anarchy, 37, 78
Arab League, 77
Arab Spring, 119
aristocracy
    Aristotle and, 37, 69
    Plato and, 37
Aristotle, 81, 94, 95, 117
    categories of state activity,
        84–85
    typology of government,
        37–38, 69
Articles of Confederation, 11–12
Atatürk, Kemal, 64, 68
autocratic versus nonautocratic
    rule, 51–54, 86

C

cities, as subnational political
    systems, 26–31
city and local government,
    29–30, 81–84
civil services, 114–115
command economy, 98
Commonwealth, the
    (Commonwealth of
    Nations), 11, 12–13
Commune of Paris, 117, 118
communism, 19, 64, 67, 109, 131
confederations and federations,
    9–14
Constitution, U.S., 11, 22, 46, 109

constitutional democracy, 51, 52,
    53–54, 67, 70–73, 88, 125
constitutional government, 60,
    70–73, 86–87
constitutional prescription,
    succession by, 46–47, 48
constitutions, 53–54, 58–59, 70, 85
coup d'etat, 49–50, 129, 131, 133

D

democracy
    Mosca and, 43
    Plato and, 37
despotism, 39
dictatorship, 64–68

E

economy, regulation of as func-
    tion of government, 104–107
education, and government,
    99–100
election, succession by, 47–48
empires, 2–5, 15, 94, 116
European Union, 13–14, 78, 102
executive division of govern-
    ment, 86–89

F

fascism, 42, 67
federal systems, 19–22
federations, 10
Ferrero, Guglielmo, 40
feudalism, 74, 94–95
force, succession by, 45, 47, 48–51

S

self-preservation, as function of government, 99–102
Settlement, Act of, 45, 46
Soviet Union, 60, 101
  collapse/dissolution of, 15, 75, 77–78
  individual rights and, 108–109
  as totalitarian dictatorship, 67
stability and instability, causes of in government, 116–126
Stalin, Joseph, 64, 67, 109
structural revision of political systems, 129
subnational political systems, 22–24
  cities, 26–31
  regions, 31–35
  tribal communities, 22–24
  villages and rural communities, 24–26
succession
  classification of government by mode of, 44–54
  by constitutional prescription, 46–47
  by election, 47–48
  by force, 48–51
  by hereditary succession, 45–46
supervision and resolution of conflicts, as function of government, 102–104
supranational political systems, 2–14
  confederations and federations, 9–14
  empires, 2–5
  leagues, 5–7

T

Tennessee Valley Authority, 34–35, 112
timocracy, Plato and, 37
totalitarian regimes, 50, 52–53, 54, 64, 67, 71, 86, 123
tribal communities, as subnational political systems, 22–24
tyranny, 60
  Aristotle and, 37

U

unitary nation-states, 17–19
United Nations, 5, 8–9, 15, 102
United States
  constitutional arrangement and, 59, 60, 71–73
  legislature of, 89, 90–91
  political executives in, 86, 87–89
  succession by constitutional prescription in, 46
  system of checks and balances, 85–86

V

villages and rural communities, as subnational political systems, 24–26

W

war, and self-preservation, 101
Weber, Max, classification system of, 40